P9-DHQ-100

EARTHWORKS AND BEYOND

EARTHWORKS

ABBEVILLE PRESS · PUBLISHERS · NEW YORK

AND BEYOND

CONTEMPORARY ART IN THE LANDSCAPE

JOHN BEARDSLEY

Editor: Nancy Grubb
Art director: Howard Morris
Designer: Robin Fox
Picture researcher: Amelia Jones
Production manager: Dana Cole

Cover: Walter De Maria. *The Lightning Field,* 1974–77. See plates 58, 59.
Title page: Alan Wood. *Fences,* part of *Ranch,* 1983. See plates 125–28.
Front end papers: James Pierce. *Earthwoman,* 1976–77. See plate 66.
Back end papers: Andy Goldsworthy. *Snowball in Trees,* Lancashire, 1980.

Marginal numbers in the text refer to works illustrated in this volume.

Library of Congress Cataloging in Publication Data

Beardsley, John.
   Earthworks and beyond.

   Bibliography: p.
   Includes index.
    1. Earthworks (Art)   2. Avant-garde (Aesthetics)—20th century. I. Title.
N6494.E27B4 1984   709'.04'076   83-21424
ISBN 0-89659-422-X
ISBN 0-89659-465-3 (pbk.)

Copyright © 1984 by Cross River Press, Ltd. All rights reserved under International and Pan-American Copyright Conventions. No part of this book may be reproduced or utilized in any form or by any means, electronic or mechanical, including photocopying, recording, or by any information storage and retrieval system, without permission in writing from the Publisher. Inquiries should be addressed to Abbeville Press, Inc., 505 Park Avenue, New York 10022. First edition.

Printed in Japan

Acknowledgments

Portions of Chapter 3 were first published in the Fall 1982 issue of *Art Journal,* "Earthworks: Past and Present." I am grateful to Rose Weil, Managing Editor, for permission to draw from that source. Reuben Rainey, Chairman of the Division of Landscape Architecture in the School of Architecture at the University of Virginia, was my guide in a study of the monuments in landscape design of the past. Such mastery as I can display of this historical material is largely to his credit. Pam Lawson, who has assisted me on so many projects before, was there to help this time as well. Nancy Grubb, my editor at Abbeville Press, helped shape my thoughts into a more coherent and articulate whole. Amy Jones managed the unwieldy task of researching photographs. I am grateful to both of them. This text touches upon many artists, though perhaps none in sufficient depth to please any but the most agreeable of them. Yet without exception, the artists I have had occasion to speak with have answered my queries with good cheer. Their cooperation is much appreciated. In the solitude of writing, friends assume even more than their usual measure of importance. Stephanie Ridder and Jane Livingston both provided needed reassurance at critical moments. Be it as it may an insufficient gesture of thanks, it is to them that this book is dedicated. J.B.

CONTENTS

1. Stonehenge is a megalithic monument (c. 2000 B.C.) on the Salisbury Plain in Wiltshire, England. Although its precise purpose remains a mystery, it is presumed by many to have served both religious and astronomical functions.

INTRODUCTION

Along with the human figure, the landscape has proved the most enduring of artistic inspirations. Only in this century has the enthusiasm for its depiction waned in the face of the technological preoccupations believed to be more appropriate to our time and the unyielding ascendancy of abstract art. Yet old enthusiasms linger even in the midst of change, and little is made that does not bear some conscious or unwitting reference to the past. In the artistic revisions that followed the cultural turbulence and social unrest of the late 1960s, it is not surprising that the landscape reappeared as inspiration for a number of the best artists of the day, nor that it resulted in some of the most astonishing and difficult art yet to be seen. A traditional subject, the landscape was nevertheless treated in a most untraditional way. Rather than representing it in paint on canvas or in rhythms of steel, a handful of artists chose to enter the landscape itself, to use its materials and work with its salient features. They were not depicting the landscape, but engaging it; their art was not simply *of* the landscape, but *in* it as well.

The first works of this kind — by Michael Heizer, Robert Smithson, Walter De Maria, and Robert Morris — have come to be known as "earthworks" or "land art." Their physical presence in the landscape itself distinguishes them from other, more portable forms of sculpture. But the involvement with landscape goes even deeper than that: most of these works are inextricably bound to their sites, and take as a large part of their content a relationship with the specific characteristics of their particular surroundings. While most of them could have been made in any one of a number of similar places, the important point is that the boundaries between them and their settings are not at all clear. These are not discrete objects, intended for isolated appraisal, but fully engaged elements of their respective environments, intended to provide an inimitable experience of a certain

place for both the artist and the viewer.

Most writings in the relatively limited literature on recent art in the landscape have been restricted to this rather self-consciously avant-garde episode in the late 1960s and early '70s. My first treatment of the subject, in the catalog of the exhibition *Probing the Earth: Contemporary Land Projects*,[1] was not really a departure from this doctrinal approach, although the inclusion of Harvey Fite and James Pierce — two artists who might have been described as "eccentrics" or "mere gardeners" in those less tolerant times — did bring a somewhat expanded focus to that effort. They were testament to the fact that land art was more diverse a phenomenon than the orthodoxies of the art scene would then have indicated.

Since that time, the forms of art in the landscape have proliferated dramatically. Only sculptures in earth and sod can properly be described as earthworks; we now have poetry gardens, artist-designed parks, architectural structures, and sculptures in concrete and steel, all of them in the landscape and all of them demonstrating a deliberate and insistent relationship with their settings. As well, we have artists exploring the landscape and bringing back testimony of their efforts in the form of photographic works and small-scale sculptures. At the same time, my increased exposure to the subject has strengthened my conviction that this art, though radical in its time, can be understood as the latest expression of an artistic impulse that is virtually ageless.

In consequence, this publication aspires to considerably more catholic an exposition of the subject than most, in the hope of securing for art in the landscape a more sympathetic reading from a greater number of people. The fact is that there are many more artists creating many more works in the landscape than can possibly receive scrutiny here, but as wide a range as feasible will be discussed. A bias must be confessed, however, for works

2. Arnaldo Pomodoro (b. 1926). *Drawing of Graveyard*, 1973. Colored pencil on paper; 19¹¹⁄₁₆ x 27⅛ in. Collection of the artist.

that aspire to at least some measure of permanence. Given the long history of artistic interchange between Britain and America, particularly in landscape painting, I have chosen to focus on art from these two countries. But this focus does exclude certain work: the park projects of the Frenchman Jean-Pierre Raynaud, the photographic manipulations of landscape by the Dutch artist Jan Dibbets, 2* and the plaza and cemetery designs of the Italian Arnaldo Pomodoro, for example.

My approach here is in equal parts reportorial and interpretive; as befits a contemporary subject, my observations are intended more to advance than to conclude critical debate on the subject. From a discussion of the American avant-garde, which confirmed the widespread reengagement with landscape in the late 1960s, the commentary moves out to the contemporary English response, back to traditions and twentieth-century antecedents, and forward to sited sculpture and the application of landscape art to the improve-

ment of public spaces — two things that have caught fire in the last few years.

Behind this text are several basic presumptions. The first is that a people's relationship to landscape is one of the most significant expressions of culture, in many respects equal in importance to the relationship to the sacred. Indeed, the two are not so dissimilar: Ralph Waldo Emerson spoke for many in his own generation and ours when he wrote that "the noblest ministry of nature is to stand as the apparition of God."² The grandest achievements of nineteenth-century American landscape painting — by Frederic Church, Thomas Cole, and Albert Bierstadt, among others — spring from this philosophical ground. Witness, too, the William H. Jackson photograph and the Thomas Moran painting of the Mountain of the Holy Cross, a peak in Colorado with deep, snow-filled crevices in the shape of a cross near its summit. These are reverential depictions of the symbol of the Passion made manifest in nature, according with the notion that the landscape itself has sacred qualities and reveals the Divinity.

The landscape is rich with man-made forms that have been offered in tribute. Prehistoric remains are merely the best known: Stonehenge, for example, whose purpose we imagine to be a pagan decoding of terrestrial and astronomical mysteries. In seventeenth-century France, the imposition of Cartesian geometry on the landscape — as at Vaux-le-Vicomte or Versailles — expressed all the bravura of an age that believed that in simple geometric shapes lay the key to the intelligible order of the universe. And in eighteenth-century England came that most remarkable episode in British intellectual history, when many of the nation's greatest thinkers — from prime ministers to poets — were engaged in the formation of gardens and vast landscaped parks that conformed to an arcadian ideal. Their goal in many instances was nothing less than the re-creation

1

2

*Marginal numbers refer to works illustrated in this volume.

3

3. Like the more famous Great Serpent Mound at Chillicothe, this vast geometrical earthwork at Newark, Ohio, is associated with the Hopewell Indian culture, which flourished in Ohio from about 1000 B.C. to A.D. 700. Photograph by James Pierce.

4. The Bronx River Parkway was built in the 1930s as part of a network of scenic links between New York City and its suburbs.

4

of a prelapsarian paradise. The landscapes at Stowe, Stourhead, and Castle Howard are only three among the almost innumerable creations of that era, a time when England acquired the picturesque appearance that persists in large measure to this day.

The efforts of our own time must seem mundane by comparison, as they are seen without the romanticizing haze of temporal distance. They are less mysterious, because both their method and their motive are better known. Neither can most of the recent works hope to attain the scale and majestic ambitions of the creations of those more imperial ages. Yet the human imagination is no less vivid or powerful than before. The contemporary works derive a great poignance from a purpose similar to that of their antecedents: to reveal the world to us anew, to combine symbolic form with the landscape in the creation of differentiated and evocative places. Some of the most remarkable of these works are arguably sacred or at least transcendent in intention, in that they assert a nonanthropocentric view of the world: they are attempts to reconcile humans with the natural environment and its implicitly sacrosanct character. At their best, they are carefully construed physical environments for the sensuous apprehension of form, while at the same time they seek to reveal the extraordinary in both the landscape and the human spirit. These are consecrated spaces for a wilfully secular era.

My second presumption is a corollary of the first. It is that the entire history of form building in the landscape is the foundation for this contemporary work. Indian mounds and cliff dwellings in this country, temple gardens in Japan, Roman and Renaissance villas in Italy as well as the creations referred to above compose a vocabulary of forms and attitudes that is unavoidably influential. The last century in this country has witnessed a considerable enlargement of this repertory, from picturesque public parks, suburbs, golf

courses, and cemeteries to the utilitarian landscape of highways, telephone poles, and roadside advertising. While few of the contemporary projects are direct counterparts of these antecedents, echoes do reverberate across the years. Only some of these correspondences will be detailed here: they are too many to enumerate them all. Suffice it to say that historical references are nearly universal, and that this is all for the best. A certain allusiveness cannot help but enrich the content and effect of a contemporary work, while it remains unmistakably of our own time.

A third underlying presumption is that in the last decade and a half the distinctions between sculpture and other forms of artistic activity have blurred. This is particularly pronounced in the case of art in the landscape, which only sometimes has the formally distinct character of conventional sculpture. At

5

6

5, 6. The Pebble Beach Golf Course, overlooking the Pacific Ocean near Monterey,
California, occupies one of the most dramatic
natural settings of any course in the world.
Designed by California State Amateur Cham-
pion Jack Neville with the assistance of
Douglas Grant, it opened for play in 1919.

The last of my presumptions merits a text
all its own, for it concerns a signal feature of
our culture. Americans are afflicted with a
profound ambivalence toward nature, manifest in a seemingly irresolvable conflict between the impulse to exploit the landscape
with ever more sophisticated tools and the
urge to nurture and protect such little as is
left of the natural world, not only for its
beauty, but also for its morally and spiritually
uplifting effect. As long ago as the early 1780s,
no less a chronicler of American life than
Thomas Jefferson complained that rapacious
farming practices were destroying the quality
of the soil. Even then, repeated cultivation of
tobacco without crop rotation was depleting
the soil of essential nutrients, resulting in
ever greater exertion on the part of its pro-
ducers and ever dwindling returns. Poverty
and malnourishment were its rewards. Tobacco growing, Jefferson asserted, "is a culture productive of infinite wretchedness."[3]
There is some irony in this observation, for
Jefferson was one of the most ardent pro-
moters of the agrarian ideal, with all its links
to contemporaneous British ideas of creating
a rural Elysium. "Those who labor in the earth
are the chosen people of God," he wrote, "if
ever He had a chosen people; whose breasts
He has made His peculiar deposit for substantial and genuine virtue."[4]

Jefferson's ideal agrarian world was not
composed of solitary individuals; it was a society of small landholders whose political and
social interactions were facilitated, even per-
fected, by their rural residence. His attitude
was distinctly antiurban, but still modestly
gregarious.[5] Henry David Thoreau, on the
other hand, revered nature as an escape from
society altogether — urban and rural alike. "I
wish to speak a word for nature, for absolute
freedom and wildness, as contrasted with a
freedom and culture merely civil — to regard
man as an inhabitant, or a part and parcel of
nature, rather than a member of society. I
wish to make an extreme statement, if so I

other times it has the impalpability of empty
space or the evanescence of performance.
With the even more recent appearance of
artist-designed parks and collaborations between artists and architects or artists and
landscape architects has come a still more
pronounced merging or at least overlap of intentions, so much so that questions have
arisen as to the identity of recent works in the
landscape as art. This issue is at once too
large and too fruitless to tackle. For the purposes of this text, an arbitrary distinction is
made between the creations of the artist and
those of the landscape architect; practical
considerations preclude a discussion of the
latter, with one exception (see chapter 4).

7. The Long Meadow at Prospect Park in Brooklyn, like Central Park in Manhattan, is one of the triumphs of the nineteenth-century landscape architects Frederick Law Olmsted and Calvert Vaux.

7

may make an emphatic one, for there are enough champions of civilization."[6] As artists began their headlong rush into the landscape in the late 1960s, it was perhaps Thoreau who was their most obvious guide, in his apparent extremism and his rejection of the world "merely civil."

Yet as this art has developed, it has moved away from the romantic and rejectionist postures of Thoreau toward the more pragmatic, socially engaged attitudes of Jefferson. The latter's early recognition that the landscape was in need of protection and restoration has been followed by several overlapping episodes of vigorous conservation. One of these, in the latter half of the nineteenth century, gave rise to the National Park System which, together with the phenomenal spread of the urban and wholly public park, might be considered America's most distinguished contribution to the history of landscape design. Another episode occurred in the 1930s with the establishment of the Civilian Conservation Corps and the consequent burgeoning of the state park system. A third, still more vigorous and controversial, began in the 1960s and continues even now. The preservation of wilderness areas, the passage of the Strip Mine Reclamation Act, and the Alaska Lands Bill are among its major accomplishments. This conservationist impulse finds a parallel in the efforts of artists who use their work as a means of restoring environmental devastation in both the city and the country.

But if these artists draw on an impulse that is rooted in a rich and diverse tradition, they find in Frederick Law Olmsted and Calvert Vaux, designers of Central Park in Manhattan and Prospect Park in Brooklyn, their most eloquent forebears. By the mid-nineteenth century, these men had recognized the social benefit of improved environmental design and outdoor recreational spaces in urban and rural areas. There is hardly an aspect of the beneficent environment in America — from single urban parks and metropolitan and national park systems to planned communities and college campuses—that does not owe its success, at least in part, to Olmsted in particular.[7] His work reflects a more widespread shift among his contemporaries away from the antiurban pronouncements of Jefferson and Thoreau to an engagement with the ever more pressing and distinctly urban problems that accompanied industrialization. To the extent that contemporary artists seek to improve the environment through land reclamation or the creation of parks, they are the inheritors of the reformist spirit of the mid-nineteenth century.

Yet the fundamental ambivalence that characterizes our national attitude toward nature is never far from any of the works I will discuss here. Indeed, some combine the reverential desire to reveal all the grandeur and mystery of the earth with the inevitable desire to use and abuse it. This is just one of the complexities of recent art works in the landscape. Some appear to be wilfully modern, in the sense of employing a reductive and frankly nonallusive vocabulary, yet they speak with an ancient voice. Conversely, some are deliberately historicist, but look entirely contemporary. Some are vast and very palpable, but seldom seen except in photographs. Some are so discreet in form or utilitarian in function that they remain unrecognized as art. Originally thought to be radical and antiurban in character, many of these works are now celebrated for their socially constructive and distinctly pro-urban motives. And while thus emphatically of this world, they frequently aspire to the quality of a revelation. Such is the character of recent art in the landscape that it resounds with paradox.

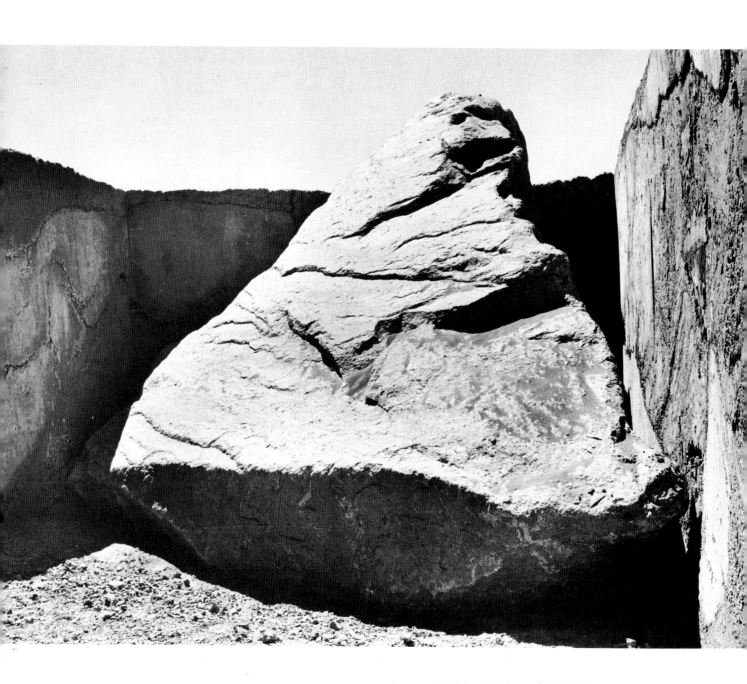

8. Michael Heizer (b. 1944). *Displaced-Replaced Mass*, detail, 1969. Three granite masses in concrete-lined depressions; overall: 900 x 400 x 13 ft. Silver Springs, Nevada (dismantled). Commissioned by Robert Scull.

1. MONUMENT AND ENVIRONMENT: THE AVANT-GARDE, 1966–1976

Michael Heizer, born in Berkeley in 1944, had by the late 1960s a high sense of mission for his sculpture. "Art had to be radical," he asserted recently. "It had to become American."[8] Much is implied in his terse statement. A Californian, he felt that sculpture needed to express the character and scale of the great Western landscapes. In an era of space exploration, and of social unrest caused by an unpopular war and racial antagonisms, he felt that art needed to look new, nonconformist, and not at all complacent. Further, it had to shake its dependence on European models, those refined objects in the tradition of Rodin and Brancusi that seemed then to be exhaling their last gasp in the form of Minimalist sculpture. Heizer's antidote was to throw off nearly all the conventions of recent three-dimensional art in favor of environmental projects.

Heizer shared in a then widespread notion that the art world was afflicted with a too grand preciosity, that artworks were valued only as commodities, and that they were limited by their preoccupation with strictly formal concerns. In 1969 Heizer decried what he perceived to be a surfeit of objects of this kind, and their seemingly inescapable associations with the marketplace: "The position of art as malleable barter-exchange item falters as the cumulative economic structure gluts. The museums and collections are stuffed, the floors are sagging, but the real space exists."[9] In the Western deserts, Heizer said that he found "that kind of unraped, peaceful, religious space artists have always tried to put in their work."[10] And he provided a blunt explanation of the differences between those works of the urban marketplace that he censured and a work in the landscape. "The intrusive, opaque object refers to itself. It has little exterior reference. It is rigid and blocks space. It is a target. An incorporative work is aerated, part of the material of its place and refers beyond itself."[11]

These ideas formed a part of the currency of artistic discourse by the late '60s. A shared enthusiasm for environmental work provided the basis of a friendship between Heizer and Walter De Maria; Heizer was also friendly with the many artists who gathered at the bar at Max's Kansas City in New York, including Robert Smithson, Nancy Holt, and Carl Andre. By the time Heizer was introduced to Smithson in 1968, he had already executed some ten temporary works in the Western deserts — trenches, motorcycle drawings, and dispersals of soil from moving vehicles and pigments into the wind. His landscape works had begun in 1967, when he sank an open cube into the ground in the Sierra Nevada, the first element in a projected four-part sculpture to be called *NESW* after the four cardinal directions. Heizer and De Maria drove across the country together inspecting potential work sites, and Heizer was on hand to help when De Maria produced his first Western work in April of 1968: two parallel lines a mile long laid down in chalk on the Mojave Desert in California. That summer, Smithson and Holt joined Heizer in Nevada, where he was working on a series of works called the *Nine Nevada Depressions*. A photograph taken by Holt shows Smithson helping to dig a trench for *Isolated Mass/ Circumflex*, giving him an early experience of working in the Western landscape.[12] Heizer's family boasted several geologists who had been active throughout the West, and there is no doubt that he was a fount of information about where to work and how to secure land by lease. But beyond that, these artists were united by a common assault on sculptural conventions. "It was a beautiful moment," Heizer recalled. "There was a lot of potential."

Heizer executed the first of his works entirely on his own initiative, without any sponsorship. By 1968, however, he had enlisted the financial aid of collector Robert Scull, who commissioned both the *Nine Nevada Depressions* and three works called *Displaced-*

9

10

9. Michael Heizer. *Isolated Mass/Circumflex*, no. 9 of the *Nine Nevada Depressions*, 1968. Excavation: 120 x 12 x 1 ft. Massacre Dry Lake, Nevada (deteriorated). Commissioned by Robert Scull.

10. Michael Heizer. *Double Negative*, 1969–70. 1,500 x 50 x 30 ft. Near Overton, Nevada. Collection of Virginia Dwan.

11. Michael Heizer. *Complex One/City*, 1972–76. Concrete, granite, and earth; 110 x 140 x 23½ ft. Collection of Virginia Dwan and the artist.

11

Replaced Mass (all 1969). For the latter, huge slabs of granite from the High Sierra were brought down to the Nevada desert and set in concrete-lined depressions in the ground. At the same time, dealer Virginia Dwan was taking an interest in Heizer's work. He had shown her a portfolio of photographs of his Western works in 1968, and she had included him, along with Smithson and Robert Morris, in her *Earthworks* exhibition that fall. Next she offered him a solo exhibition. He agreed, on the understanding that the exhibition would not be limited to the gallery. With her backing, he returned to Nevada, secured a site on the Mormon Mesa, hired contractors and earthmoving equipment, and began
10 work on a piece he was to title *Double Negative*: two cuts in the mesa surface facing each

other across a deep indentation in the escarpment. Heizer had excavated the thirty-foot-wide cuts to a depth of forty-two feet when he ran short of cash. He called Dwan for additional help; she came to Nevada to see the piece and gave him the authorization to finish the work. It was deepened to 50 feet, and expanded to a total length of 1,500.

Double Negative took the art world by surprise. Its debut in a Dwan Gallery exhibition in early 1970 was hardly placid. One critic subsequently wrote that "it proceeds by marring the very land, which is what we have just learned to stop doing."[13] Referring to Heizer's work several years later, another asserted that "earth art, with very few exceptions, not only doesn't improve upon its natural environment, it destroys it."[14] If these criticisms are

12. Teotihuacán, the largest of
the religious and commercial centers of
ancient America, was built between A.D. 300
and 900. Laid out in a grid, it is dominated
by the Pyramid of the Sun.

justified, they are also incomplete. The aggressiveness of Heizer's intervention in the landscape of the Mormon Mesa must be seen in the context of the entirely new syntax he was proposing for sculpture. Rather than being a form that occupies space, with a surface delineating the limits of an internal volume, *Double Negative* is composed of space itself: it is a void. Although massive in scale, it is barely palpable. The two sunken enclosures call to each other across the great chasm of the escarpment, providing an experience of vastness conveyed through the arrangement of space that is compellingly distinct from the intrusive, space-occupying character of traditional monuments. One is *inside* this piece. And while that is typical of architecture and landscape design, it is certainly distinct from most previous sculpture.

Some years later, Heizer sought to clarify his intentions, which many found disturbingly radical: both antiart and antiestablishment. He was realistic enough to acknowledge that the economics of the art world represented an unassailable bulwark. By then it was also clear that earthworks relied on fairly conventional forms of patronage. He recognized that the importance of his work lay not in what it rejected, but in what it offered instead. "I was never out to destroy the gallery system or the aesthetic object," he explained. "I wasn't trying to make impermanent works—I was just doing the best I could with the tools I could afford. I'm not a radical. In fact, I'm going backward. I like to attach myself to the past."[15] That past is frankly archaeological. Heizer's father was a noted archaeologist and provided his son with an early introduction to the monuments of the past, particularly those of pre-Columbian America. The three *Displaced-Replaced Mass* sculptures allude to the moving of the great monoliths that form the Colossi of Memnon in the Valley of the Kings in Egypt, which Heizer's father had studied, as well as to the giant "wandering rocks" that were hauled

hundreds of miles around the desert in pre-Inca Bolivia.

Heizer's next major Western work after *Double Negative* was likewise a deft blending of archaeological references with his spare, geometric idiom. Located in south-central Nevada, *Complex One* (1972–76) is a long mound of earth with sloping sides and trapezoidal ends; it is some 140 feet long and nearly 24 feet high. The western face — the front — includes a group of concrete "framing elements," which read as a continuous band when viewed directly from the front of the piece, but break up as one moves to the sides. Some of them are attached to the mound itself, while others are set a good distance from it; some lie flat while others are cantilevered. The central unit at the top, for example, is thirty feet long and hangs thirty feet out from the front, producing constantly changing shadows across the face of the mound. Heizer has identified the snake bands lining the ball court at Chichen Itza in the Yucatán as a source for these framing elements, while the mound itself relates to Egyptian mastabas, ancient tombs that predate the pyramids.[16]

Complex One is just the first of a group of massive works planned for the site. Heizer has excavated the area directly in front of *Complex One*, creating an enormous depression around which the other works will be placed. One of them, a long sloping mound with an austerely geometric façade, is presently under construction. *Complex One* will thus eventually be one side of a square, forming an enclosed precinct rather like the one in front of the Pyramid of the Moon at Teotihuacán near Mexico City, or the great plazas at Monte Alban in the Mexican state of Oaxaca, or Tikal in Guatemala. Doubtless the ceremonial associations of these pre-Columbian works will be felt, lending Heizer's complex an air not only of history, but of incompletely understood ritual as well.

When finally completed, Heizer's precinct

13. Walter De Maria (b. 1935). *Las Vegas Piece*, 1969. Overall length: three miles. Tula Desert, Nevada.

will exclude all views of the surrounding landscape. The works will completely enclose the viewer, who will stand well below ground level. Part of the motivation for this, Heizer explains, is to clear up any remaining confusion about the intent of his work. "It's about art, not about landscape," he insists. Some association with the landscape is unavoidable: the works are, after all, situated in a flat basin whose distant mountain ranges echo the long, ground-hugging, rough character of Heizer's mounds. But the point is well taken, reminding us that the purpose of these works is to create art, not simply to make a statement about the landscape. Indeed, when he first began work on these additional elements, Heizer had some cause for wanting to exclude the adjacent landscape: it was then being studied as a possible site for an MX missile base.

One imagines that Heizer's quadrangle will have more of the character of conventional monuments than his *Double Negative*. The elements will be massive and occupy space emphatically. Yet though the parts may be large in size, they can never be truly large in relation to the scale of the surrounding basins and ranges. And the excavation between them will be a part of, if not the principal element of, the work. The parts will define an environment for which we, the viewers, are the center, rather than occupying the center themselves as conventional monuments do. Heizer will thus have remained true to his original intentions for his art in the landscape: to offer in place of the rarefied and self-referential barter-object an art that is richly allusive in content and environmental in character.

13 In 1969, the year after he drew his chalk lines in the company of Heizer, De Maria was back in the West to execute his *Las Vegas Piece*, four shallow cuts made by the six-foot blade of a bulldozer in the central Nevada desert. These cuts form a square with half-mile sides, with two of the sides extending

another half a mile at opposite corners. All are oriented north to south or east to west. This is a piece that yields its charms slowly. While one eventually comes to learn its configuration, it is never entirely visible. Instead, it presents itself as a series of options, invitations to move along a horizontal plane in the four cardinal directions. De Maria's lines are compelling: one feels that one's progress along them is somehow involuntary. Yet with this comes a feeling of relief that there is a delineated path on which to progress, in a landscape where one might otherwise wander aimlessly. As one walks the piece, its monotony is at first soothing and finally invigorating as one realizes the completeness with which one has experienced both the work and its surrounding landscape. This creation of dimensional, directional space with an understated, almost immaterial means reappeared in De Maria's later *Lightning Field* 59,60 (discussed in chapter 3).

For his part, Smithson took advantage of his Western visit with Heizer in 1968 to collect for his "Nonsites": sculptures composed of materials gathered outdoors, set in geometric containers, and frequently exhibited with maps or photographs of the sites from which they were taken. Smithson devoted much of that year to these sculptures, amassing sand from the New Jersey Pine Barrens in the winter, for example, limestone from Franklin, New Jersey, in the spring, and pumice and cinders from Mono Lake, California, in the summer. The resulting works were indoor evocations of outdoor locations, establishing what Smithson termed a dialectic between site — the outdoor source of the earth materials — and nonsite — the sculpture in its dissociated setting, functioning as a signifier of the absent site. Smithson produced a variation on these the following year, a group of rock salt and mirror pieces for the *Earth Art* exhibition at Cornell University in Ithaca, New York.[17] Like the subsequent *Rocks and Mirror Square* (1969), these used reflection to

14. Robert Smithson (1938–1973). *Texas Overflow (Sulphur Version)*, 1970. Pencil and crayon on paper; 24 x 19 in. Estate of Robert Smithson, courtesy of John Weber Gallery, New York.

15. Robert Smithson. *Spiral Jetty*, 1970. Black basalt and limestone rocks and earth; length: 1,500 ft. Great Salt Lake, Utah. Estate of Robert Smithson.

phur, contrasting the viscous with the solid, the black with the yellow. But it was in 1970 that Smithson made his major mark on the landscape. Like Heizer, he enlisted the sponsorship of Virginia Dwan, went West, and produced his *Spiral Jetty*: 1,500 linear feet of black basalt and limestone rocks and earth that curls into the Great Salt Lake, Utah, at a site Smithson leased on its northeastern shore.   15–17

"A sense of place" has become the dominant cliché in describing the effect of recent works in the landscape. It alludes, however unconsciously, to the celebrated admonition of the eighteenth-century English poet Alexander Pope, who advised that one "Consult the Genius of the Place in all."[18] In other words, one should design in conformity with nature, drawing out the best characteristics of the site, and thereby enhance the work created upon it. *Spiral Jetty*, as revealed in Smithson's own writings, provides a particularly lucid example of this correspondence between art work and site. Smithson was a prolific if occasionally confused writer;[19] indeed, it was as much through his numerous essays as through his sculptures that he was largely responsible for engaging the attentions of a large and influential art-world audience — including curators, critics, and magazine editors — for the landscape activities of the avant-garde.

Two years after the completion of the *Spiral Jetty*, Smithson published an essay about the work.[20] In it he detailed finding the site, his reactions to it, and how they resulted in this particular piece. It is an illuminating account and worth quoting at length. He described driving down a wide valley toward the Salt Lake, "which resembled an impassive faint violet sheet held captive in a stoney matrix, upon which the sun poured down its crushing light." He reached the lake at a place called Rozel Point, where industrial wreckage and abandoned vehicles bore witness to recent unsuccessful efforts to extract oil from

simulate the scale of the out-of-doors.

The same year — 1969 — Smithson began producing his works in the landscape itself. He composed a sequence of temporary mirror pieces on the beach and in the jungle of the Yucatán, and poured asphalt down the side of a quarry outside of Rome, simulating a lava flow. One of Smithson's many drawings, *Texas Overflow*, subsequently proposed another, potentially more intriguing poured work. Into the center of a circular mount, ringed with brilliant yellow sulphur rocks, hot asphalt would have been poured and allowed to run down between the sul-   14

tar deposits. "A great pleasure arose from seeing all those incoherent structures. This site gave evidence of a succession of man-made systems mired in abandoned hopes." This infatuation with decay and industrial ruin had a great influence on Smithson (though it was more particularly manifest in the reclamation projects that postdated the *Spiral Jetty*). He continued:

About one mile north of the oil seeps I selected my site. Irregular beds of limestone dip gently eastward, massive deposits of black basalt are broken over the peninsula, giving the region a shattered appearance. It is one of the few places on the lake where the water comes right up to the mainland. Under shallow pinkish water is a network of mud cracks supporting the jig-saw puzzle that composes the salt flats. As I looked at the site, it reverberated out to the horizons only to suggest an immobile cyclone while flickering light made the entire landscape appear to quake. A dormant earthquake spread into the fluttering stillness, into a spinning sensation without movement. This site was a rotary that enclosed itself in an immense roundness. From that gyrating space emerged the possibility of the Spiral Jetty.

If the spiral form of Smithson's jetty was derived from a reading of the local topography, it had additional relevance to the site. The salt crystals that coat the rocks on the water's edge form in the shape of a spiral. "Each cubic salt crystal echoes the Spiral Jetty in terms of the crystal's molecular lattice. . . . The Spiral Jetty could be considered one layer within the spiraling crystal lattice, magnified trillions of times." In addition, while visiting the region Smithson had learned of a legend that the Great Salt Lake was connected to the ocean by an underground channel, which revealed itself in the middle of the lake as an enormous whirlpool. The spiral was thus a key not only to the mac-roscopic world, but the microscopic and mythological as well.

Smithson was drawn to the Great Salt Lake by the knowledge that it contained a micro-organism that colored the water pink. He had read of similar lakes in South America and was eager to see this phenomenon for himself. One knows from his writings that he was invigorated by the kind of desolation encountered at this site: "A bleached and fractured world surrounds the artist. To organize this mess of corrosion into patterns, grids and subdivisions is an aesthetic process that has scarcely been touched."[21] Smithson's vocabulary — *shattered, fractured, corrosion* — reveals his preoccupation with entropy as a measure of disorder. The spiral — open, irreversible, "coming from nowhere, going nowhere," as Smithson put it[22] — accords with this preoccupation. At the *Spiral Jetty*, the gyre is not widening, but falling inward: it is "matter collapsing into the lake mirrored in the shape of a spiral."[23]

After the *Spiral Jetty*, Smithson's work took a different turn. In 1971 he was invited to the Netherlands to participate in an international exhibition called *Sonsbeek 71*. Feeling that the Dutch landscape was already very cultivated and that a work of art upon it would be superfluous, he asked to work at a disrupted site instead. A virtually exhausted sand quarry that was destined to be converted into a recreation area was found for him in Emmen, in northeastern Holland. It became the location of his first effort to reclaim an industrially devastated landscape through art.

Smithson's sand quarry was composed of white and yellow sand, red and brown loam, and a blue-green pond. At one edge of the water, Smithson had a slope graded flat, a curving channel cut into it, and an arced jetty built out into the water, forming the *Broken Circle* (about 140 feet in diameter). On the slope above, *Spiral Hill* was made of overburden and a covering layer of topsoil, with a counterclockwise path of white sand that

18

wound to the top. While the latter work is not particularly distinguished for either the deftness of its execution or the originality of its form, *Broken Circle* is intriguing for its symmetry of opposites: semicircles of water and soil, canal and jetty. It is also given an enchanted quality by the huge glacial boulder that was discovered while grading the site. The boulder apparently plagued Smithson, who felt that it added an undesirable focal point to the work, but it proved too large to be moved. In the end, Smithson grew to appreciate this boulder for its associations with prehistoric burial markers found in the area.[24]

The significance of the *Broken Circle* and *Spiral Hill* lay in the incentive they gave to Smithson to pursue his pairing of art with land reclamation. "Across the country," he wrote in the aftermath of these works, "there are many mining areas, disused quarries, and polluted lakes and rivers. One practical solution for the utilization of such devasted places would be land and water re-cycling in terms of 'Earth Art.' "[25] Smithson did not entirely detest industrial activities, recognizing them as a necessary corollary of the life we have developed for ourselves. He viewed human interventions in the landscape as no more unnatural than earthquakes and typhoons. What he did take exception to, however, was the lack of sensitivity he perceived among industrialists to the visual values of the landscape, which he rightly realized were "traditionally the domain of those concerned with the arts."[26] He wrote to a host of mining companies offering his services to enhance the visual qualities of their reclamation activities. "Art can become a physical resource that mediates between the ecologist and the industrialist," he claimed, facilitating the aims of both.[27]

In two cases, Smithson's ideas received considerable elaboration, though both failed to reach fruition. In 1972 he entered into negotiations with the Hanna Coal Company, which was beginning the reclamation of a

thousand-acre site in the Egypt Valley in southeastern Ohio. Smithson proposed incorporating his earthworks not as a substitute for but an addition to the company's standard efforts, in order to add visual focus to the site and draw attention to the surrounding reclamation work. In October of that year he sent the company two drawings for a specific piece. It would have been morphologically related to *Broken Circle*, with a curved jetty embracing a semicircular cove on the shore of a lake. Paths along the shoreline would have been covered with crushed limestone, and portions of the piece would have been planted with crown vetch, a legume that aids in preventing soil erosion and restoring fertility.

Early the next year, Smithson began discussions with the Minerals Engineering Company of Denver concerning the disposition of tailings at their mine in Creede, Colorado. Tailings are the waste material that remains after the desired ore is extracted from mined rock. Because they often contain residue of valuable minerals, they are set aside in the event that future recovery becomes practicable. Smithson proposed utilizing these tailings to build a group of earthworks. Some of the waste was being flushed into basins; he suggested building a series of concentric dams down the slope of a hill, creating ponds that would gradually fill to become terraces as they received the tailings. One drawing indicated the scale at which he hoped to work: it was for a semicircular pond that would be 2,000 feet in diameter, and contain nine million tons of material deposited over twenty-five years. Two other drawings propose a *Garden of Tailings* — curved berms radiating from a common center — and a *Meandering Ring* — random piles with bulldozed pathways between them, the whole forming a circle with an open center.

It is significant that in neither of these proposals did Smithson suggest disguising entirely the postindustrial character of his site

16

17

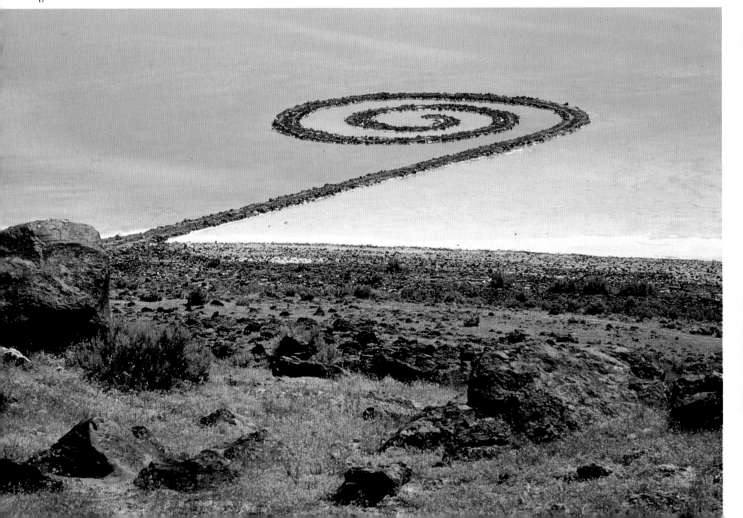

16, 17. Robert Smithson, *Spiral Jetty*. See plate 15.

18. Robert Smithson. *Broken Circle* and, on the slope above, *Spiral Hill*, 1971. Diameter of circle: 140 ft.; of hill: 75 ft. Emmen, the Netherlands.

19. Robert Smithson. *Amarillo Ramp*, 1973. Diameter: 150 ft. Amarillo, Texas. Collection of Stanley Marsh, Amarillo.

18

20. Robert Morris (b. 1931). *Observatory*, 1971; reconstructed 1977. Approximate diameter: 300 ft. Oostelijk Flevoland, the Netherlands. Collection of the Rijksdienst for IJsselmeer-polders, Lelystad.

and materials. He felt it was inappropriate to attempt to recreate a perfect landscape and endeavored instead to evolve an artistically enriched and distinctly man-made landscape that acknowledged technological use. Smithson's proposals thus have a brutally realistic character, and something of a commemorative function. His projects for tailings would have stood as memorials to industrial disruption of the landscape, and as provocations to contemplate the efficacy and necessity of our resource development policies.

Frustrated by the slow pace of negotiations with these mining companies, Smithson accepted the opportunity to work on a ranch in west Texas. He selected a site on the shore of an irrigation lake and staked out the shape of an ascending ramp forming an open circle 150 feet in diameter. While he was making a routine inspection of the planned piece from the air, the plane crashed, killing Smithson, the pilot, and a photographer. The *Amarillo Ramp* was subsequently completed by Nancy Holt and Smithson's friends Tony Shafrazi and Richard Serra. Smithson's early death effectively foreclosed further consideration of his reclamation proposals. They remain, however, his richest legacy, a source of inspiration for a host of subsequent artists.

Like Smithson, Robert Morris was invited to participate in *Sonsbeek 71*; he too had been developing his ideas for art in the landscape for several years. Among the first had been a *Project in Earth and Sod* (1966), a large grassy ring proposed for the Dallas-Fort Worth Regional Airport. Over the next several years Morris produced numerous other proposals — for serpentine mounds, spiral hills, and the like — but his invitation to Holland in 1971 was his first opportunity to see any of these works realized. The result was his *Observatory*, originally built near the Dutch coastal town of Velsen. It was razed at the conclusion of the exhibition but, largely through the efforts of its original sponsors

and with considerable Dutch governmental support, it was rebuilt in a slightly enlarged form on new land created from the vast IJsselmeer or Zuider Zee. This new land, or polder, is formed by erecting long, thick dikes and pumping out the seawater. Once the bottom of a shallow inland sea, this land is unwaveringly flat and consequently ideal for the purposes Morris had in mind.

As reconstructed in 1977, *Observatory* consists of two concentric rings of earth with an outer diameter of nearly 200 feet. The inner ring — nine feet high and seventy-nine feet in diameter — is formed of earth piled up against a circular wooden stockade. The outer circumference consists of three embankments and two canals. Entrance to the piece is gained via a triangular passage cut through the embankment to the west; a path leads from there through a break in the central enclosure. Once inside this stockade, three other openings are visible. The first looks due east along two parallel channels, each of which terminates in a ten-foot-square steel plate propped on a diagonal. The interval between these plates, as seen from within the central enclosure, marks the position of the sunrise on the equinoxes. Two other openings look thirty-seven degrees northeast and southeast, through notches on the outer embankment lined with granite boulders and marking the points of the sunrise on the summer and winter solstices, respectively.

Morris's deployment of archaic references — solar sight lines and large granite blocks — parallels Heizer's strategy at *Complex One*: to blend an empathetic historicism with a contemporary idiom. Morris was likewise disaffected from much recent art. "It seems a truism at this point," he wrote in 1971, "that the static, portable indoor art object can do no more than carry a decorative load that becomes increasingly uninteresting."[28] What interested Morris instead was not simply revealing the world to the observer, but also the conditions of perception. With an apparent nod in the direction of the phenomenology of the French philosopher Maurice Merleau-Ponty, Morris aimed at creating "a place in which the perceiving self might take measure of certain aspects of its own physical existence."[29] By creating — as at his *Observatory* — an art work that was too large or too complex to be viewed in an instant, that required the viewer to walk through and around it, Morris provided an "experience of an interaction between the perceiving body and the world which fully admits that the terms of this interaction are temporal as well as spatial, that existence is process, that the art itself is a form of behavior. . . ."[30]

In the case of the *Observatory*, this behavior leads to an awareness of how information is absorbed by the senses and combined to produce a coherent mental image of something that is impossible to comprehend instantaneously. It also leads to an awareness of the different measures of time. There is the viewer's time — the amount required to move around and comprehend the piece. Contrasted with this are times of two vastly different sorts: the far longer time of human history, implicit in the reference to neolithic monuments, and the virtually imponderable measure of astronomical time revealed

through the use of solar sight lines. The use of archaic references and the solar orientation are thus not only historicist. They also require us to acknowledge the subjectivity of our own sense of time by juxtaposing it with two more awesome and enduring measures.

Morris's emphasis on the importance of the viewer's participation in coming to know an art work is crucial to understanding his *Grand Rapids Project* as well. This work came about 22 in the aftermath of an outdoor sculpture exhibition organized by the Women's Committee of the Grand Rapids Art Museum in 1973. Entitled *Sculpture off the Pedestal*, the exhibition was intended to explore the use of a wide variety of sculptural types in different public situations. When Morris was invited to participate, he recognized this as an opportunity to focus public attention on the notion of art in the landscape. On a visit to Grand Rapids, he found a badly eroded hillside in one of the city's recreation areas. He later described this site as "in tune with my concerns for outside works — works which cooperate and do not become applied 'objects'. . . stuck onto the landscape."[31] He proposed recontouring the slope and linking the top and bottom of the hill with a pair of intersecting pathways in the shape of an X. This proposal

21. Robert Morris, *Observatory*. See plate 20.

22. Robert Morris. *Grand Rapids Project*, 1973–74. Length of ramps: 478 ft. Belknap Park, Grand Rapids, Michigan. Collection of the City of Grand Rapids.

21

was reviewed by the City Parks and Recreation Department to insure, among other things, adequate plant cover and proper drainage. The piece was then constructed in the summer and fall of 1974, with funds from the National Endowment for the Arts, the Michigan Council for the Arts, the Women's Committee of the Museum, and with "in-kind" contributions from the city.

Although the configuration of this work seems quite obvious at first glance, there are in fact subtle shifts in the grade of the slope and the length of the paths that become obvious only when experiencing the piece. Like the *Observatory*, it becomes a place for the enactment of various sorts of behavior: "runnings, walkings, viewings, crossings, waitings, meetings, coolings, heatings," among the many others that Morris mentioned in a catalog published about the project.[32]

Morris's *Grand Rapids Project* was to prove enormously significant to the future of art in the landscape in the United States. While Smithson's *Broken Circle* and *Spiral Hill* and Morris's *Observatory* came into being with government support in Holland, the *Grand Rapids Project* marked the first time that public funds had been involved in effecting a large-scale environmental work in America. From this date, the National Endowment for the Arts, the General Services Administration, and numerous state, county, and municipal organizations displayed increasing receptiveness to this sort of art. This coincided with a growing commitment among artists to the evolving public purposes of art in the landscape. Smithson's notion that artists have not only the capacity but also the social obliga-

22

23

tion to make a beneficial contribution to the use and restoration of the landscape was to win ever-wider approval as the years passed. And while projects continued to come into being entirely through private sponsorship, more and more public patrons were to accept both the aesthetic and utilitarian aims of recent art in the landscape. It is ironic that this public support began with what is certainly among the most inscrutable and, in visual terms, the least captivating works of this genre.

23   Nineteen seventy-four also saw the completion of Richard Fleischner's *Sod Maze* in Newport, Rhode Island. This too was the result of an outdoor sculpture exhibition, called *Monumenta*, which came about with partial public sponsorship. While most of the forty-one artists showed preexisting works, Fleischner created one especially for the exhibition. He selected the grounds of Château-sur-Mer, a mansion belonging to the Preservation Society of Newport County, from

among the sites made available to him. There he constructed a mounded turf maze some 142 feet in diameter and a scant 18 inches high. It has only a single path to the center, which is visible in any case because of the low relief; it therefore does not function like the deliberately puzzling topiary mazes that are the best known of the labyrinth types. Instead it relates to more ancient maze forms: those cut in the stone floors of medieval cathedrals, as at Chartres, and functioning as allegories of penance and purification (often quite literally, as penitents traversed them on their knees); and those cut in the ground — dug and low mounded — in medieval England, based perhaps on Roman models, and having an ornamental purpose. It is this sort of maze that appears in *A Midsummer Night's Dream*: "The nine men's morris is filled up with mud; / and the quaint mazes in the wanton green, / for lack of tread, are undistinguishable."

Meanwhile, the Western landscape con-

23. Richard Fleischner (b. 1944). *Sod Maze*, 1974. Sod and earth; height: 18 in., diameter: 142 ft. Newport, Rhode Island. Collection of the Preservation Society of Newport County.

24. Ant Farm (Chip Lord, Hudson Marquez, Doug Michels). *Cadillac Ranch*, 1974. 10 Cadillacs. Amarillo, Texas. Commissioned by Stanley Marsh, Amarillo.

24

tinued to blossom with art works, albeit of a very different sort. A San Francisco collective called Ant Farm — including Chip Lord, Hudson Marquez, and Doug Michels — upended 24 ten Cadillacs along Route 66 near Amarillo, Texas, in 1974. Ranging in vintage from 1948 to 1962, the cars were buried to their midsections in what can only be described as a requiem for the golden age of the American automobile. The flamboyance of this gesture has been equaled only by the work of the Bulgarian-born artist Christo. In 1971 he made his first attempt at hanging the *Valley Curtain*, a glistening orange nylon drape spanning the more than 1,300-foot width of Rifle Gap in Colorado. A gust of wind damaged the fabric, however, and final installation was delayed until the summer of 1972. Even then, a vicious windstorm shredded the *Curtain* a mere twenty-eight hours after it was unfurled from the suspension cables and anchored to the ground.

25, 26 In 1976 came Christo's *Running Fence*, by far the most publicized of the recent works in the landscape. It ran twenty-four and a half miles across the hills of Sonoma and Marin counties, leaping roads and crossing cattle pastures before plunging into the Pacific. It was composed of 2,050 panels of a white nylon fabric, each 18 feet high and 68 feet wide, held aloft by cables and hooks strung between steel poles. It graced the rolling landscape of Northern California for a brief two weeks in the middle of September, at a cost of some three million dollars raised privately through the sale of Christo's drawings and collages.

There is something undeniably captivating in the images of Christo's *Fence* snaking its way through the landscape, revealing the contours as it goes. Yet Christo was emphatic that this was not the sole content of his work. "I didn't just want a nice fence and a beautiful landscape," he said. Instead, encouraged by his knowledge of the activities of the post-Revolutionary avant-garde in Russia (acquired

25, 26. Christo (b. 1935). *Running Fence*, 1972–76. Steel poles, steel cables, and 2½ million square ft. of woven nylon; height: 18 ft., overall length: 24½ miles. Sonoma and Marin counties, California (dismantled).

26

27. Nancy Holt (b. 1938). *Sun Tunnels*, 1973–76, view from the darkened interior of one of the tunnels. Concrete; length: 18 ft., diameter: 9 ft., each pipe. Lucin, Utah. Collection of the artist.

28. Nancy Holt, *Sun Tunnels*, general view.

while an art student in Bulgaria), Christo sought a closer interaction between his art and its broader cultural context. "Just as religion was important to the Quattrocento artist," he explained, "so are economics, social problems and politics today . . . the greatest drama. Knowledge of these areas should be an important part of one's work."[33] Forty-two months were required to realize the *Running Fence*. Permission was negotiated to cross fifty-nine ranches. Eighteen public hearings were held; three sessions in the Superior Courts of California were devoted to the project; and 450 pages of environmental impact statements were prepared. These are the cultural structures that help determine the visible form of human interventions in the landscape; revealing them was at least as important a part of the *Fence* to Christo as its physical configuration. They were elaborately documented in the book and film that were produced about the project.

Despite all the public preparation, still the *Fence* ended in controversy. It had many enthusiastic partisans, but it was scorned by some for having so extravagant a price tag and no apparent purpose. Others objected to the fact that it was to cross the strip of land along the coast protected by the California Coastal Zone Commission. The commission's regulations require that at certain designated places nothing be constructed without their approval in a 1,000-foot-wide strip beginning at the tide line. Christo sought and received a permit, but the commission's decision was appealed. His permit was thus under review at the time he completed the *Fence*, bringing it the full distance into the ocean. To some, Christo's cavalier disregard of this regulation undermined the premise of his project, which was avowedly to reveal and not to circumvent the economic, social, and political structures governing the landscape.[34]

Christo's was a new form of art in the landscape: temporary, theatrical, and involving large numbers of people. When Nancy Holt completed her first major work in 1976 she continued the tradition of remote, large-scale, and durable works initiated by Heizer and Smithson. Constructed in the desert of northwestern Utah, her *Sun Tunnels* consists of four concrete pipes, each eighteen feet long and slightly over nine feet in diameter, placed in an open X configuration about fifty feet apart. They are aligned to the rising and setting of the sun on the summer and winter solstices — roughly thirty-two degrees north and south of true east and west. At sunrise and sunset on the summer and winter solstices and for about ten days before and after, the sun is visible through the pairs of pipes. Additional visual incident is brought to the piece by holes that are cut in the upper surfaces of the pipes in the shape of different constellations: Draco, Perseus, Columba, and Capricorn. These holes are variously seven to ten inches in diameter, with the size relative to the magnitude of the star to which the hole corresponds. During the day and by moonlight, spots of light move across the inside of the tunnels in the configurations of these constellations. As Holt herself has nicely explicated, "Day is turned into night, and an inversion of the sky takes place: Stars are cast down to earth, spots of warmth in cool tunnels."[35]

A surprising lyricism is achieved by Holt's rough pipes, which barely disguise their industrial origin. They provide welcome shelter, cool solace from the desert sun. Likewise, they offer a reassuring indication of direction in a trackless landscape and frame vistas within the disconcerting vastness. Holt compares the site with a passage from T. S. Eliot's *Four Quartets* (1943): "Dawn points, and another day / Prepares for heat and silence." Her *Sun Tunnels* are a dignified yet humanly scaled setting in which to experience the grand awfulness of the natural surroundings.

Two other still-unfinished works for the Western deserts were also given birth in the middle years of the 1970s. In 1974 Charles

27–29

29. Nancy Holt, *Sun Tunnels*, sunset on the summer solstice.

30. James Turrell (b. 1943). *Amba*, 1982. A temporary light installation at the Center on Contemporary Art, Seattle, Washington.

31. Roden Crater, near Flagstaff, Arizona.

29

30

31

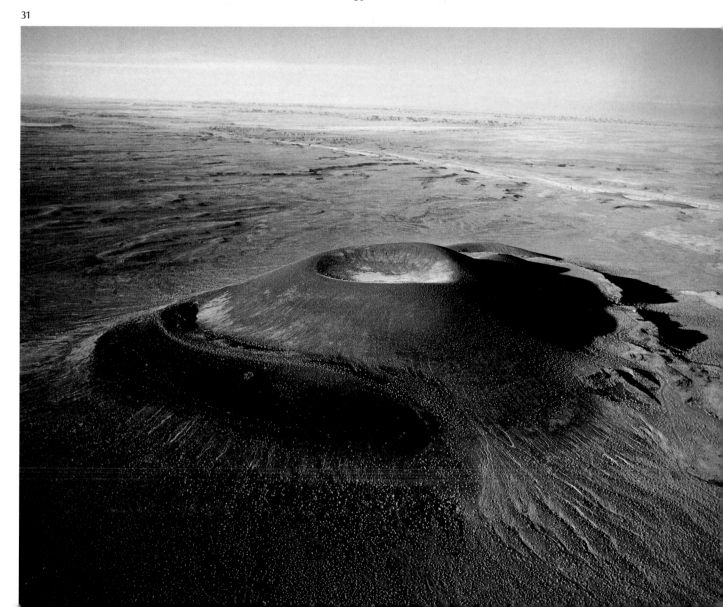

32. James Turrell. *Cut and Fill and Tunnel Alignment for Roden Crater Project*, 1980. Ink and pencil on Mylar; 36 x 72 in. Collection of the artist.

Ross found a site in the semiarid mesa country west of Albuquerque for a work to be called *Star Axis*. When completed, it will consist of a vastly elongated concrete cylinder — 200 feet long and 7 feet in diameter — rising diagonally up the escarpment of the mesa and some 50 feet into the air beyond. It will be oriented to astronomical north: the infinite extension of the earth's axis into space. Because of a wobble in the earth's rotation, the point we perceive as north changes, with a cycle of 26,000 years. At certain times in this wobble, the axis aligns quite closely with a particular star. When the Great Pyramid was built over 4,500 years ago, it was oriented to what was then the North Star, Thuban in the constellation Draco. In our own time, the earth's axis has rotated into a near alignment with Polaris. By the middle of the next century, this alignment will be almost perfect.

Star Axis is planned to demonstrate the re-lationship between Polaris and the earth's axis. At the time of their closest alignment, Polaris will describe a one-degree circle around the astronomical pole each day. Standing at the bottom of Ross's cylinder, one will look up at a one-degree circle of sky; Polaris will be seen to rotate around the rim of the opening each day. Climbing up the cylinder, one will see ever larger circles of sky, each describing the circumpolar orbit of Polaris as the earth's axis moves away from it. And from the top, one will see evidence of an entirely different phenomenon. A bow-shaped field, larger at either end than in the middle, will describe the limits of the area in which the shadow of the cylinder's tip will fall during the year. This shadow field will give evidence of the earth's seasonally varying relationship to the sun. Ross has investigated this in another form already, in a series of works called *Sunlight Convergence/Solar*

Burns: The Year Shape. Using a lens set up on the roof of his New York studio to focus sunlight, Ross allowed the sun to burn an image of its daily course onto a piece of wood. When these boards are set end to end at the conclusion of the year, they form a spiral that reverses midway. This reversing curve will be apparent in the shadow field at *Star Axis*.

It is still anyone's guess what will be the precise effect of Ross's piece. The accomplishments of James Turrell that have led up to his *Roden Crater Project*, however, give this proposed work fair promise of magic. For the past two decades, Turrell has created 30 ethereal environments in which light is perceived almost as a palpable, physical presence. Initially accomplished through the use of projected or fluorescent light cast around, through, or onto carefully arranged constructions, these pieces demonstrated how manipulated light could control or alter the perceived character of a space. The means by which Turrell accomplished this transformation were confounding, but the effects were transfixing. Room shapes were altered by light; perceived walls turned out to be voids.

Turrell has also worked with natural light, an enthusiasm that will reach an apogee with 31,32 his *Roden Crater Project*. In and around the red and black cinder cone of a long-extinct volcano near Flagstaff, Arizona, Turrell will fashion seven spaces in which to experience the changing qualities of sun and moonlight. Five will be on the outside slope of the cone, in a side vent. From there, a long tunnel will lead into a chamber at the bottom of the caldera, and finally into the bowl of the cinder cone itself. The rim of the cone will be somewhat recontoured, as will the bowl, to enhance the reception of light. Looking out from these spaces, one will be able to observe at periodic intervals what Turrell describes as "imaged events:" a moonrise here, a solstice sunset there. These will work in concert with daily fluctuations of sun and moonlight to create ever-changing perceptual environments.

Monumental in scale, yet exceedingly subtle in form, Turrell's project is like many others of the recent avant-garde. Like them, it exploits the characteristics of the surrounding landscape — its contours and materials, its ambient light — no less than its symbolic and emotional qualities. Turrell's high ambition is to reveal to us anew the extraordinary properties — physical, symbolic, and psychic — of light, one of the commonplaces of our lives. Like many other recent artists in the landscape, he aims to create an environment of rapture.

2. THE RAMBLE

In England, circumstances similar to those in the United States prevailed in the latter half of the 1960s. A group of younger artists, dissatisfied with the current forms of painting and sculpture, opted for alternatives to the precious object in environmental and performance art. Two sculptors, Richard Long and Hamish Fulton — both of whom matriculated in the mid-1960s at St. Martin's School of Art in London, then the testing ground for advanced art in Britain — led the way forward, and back, into the English landscape. But what they did when they got there displayed a sensibility quite unlike that of their American contemporaries. They barely intruded upon the landscape at all. Indeed, Fulton made no mark other than footprints and took nothing but photographs. Long also made photographs, and while he sometimes reorganized landscape elements — rocks and sticks — he did so in ways that were hardly discernible. Walking was the principal form of artistic activity for both these men.

Theirs was a sensibility no less romantic in its reveries than the American, but decidedly less heroic in its means.[36] Nourished by the long tradition of landscape veneration in Britain — in painting, literature, and garden design — the contemporary English sensibility may well find its clearest antecedent in the life and work of William Wordsworth, with his physical ramblings through the landscape of the Lake District and his poetic musings on the same. The antiheroism of the recent work is no doubt a reflection of the present-day character of the English countryside. A land more densely populated than America and without its vast open spaces, England presents fewer opportunities for grand gestures than the United States. While Smithson could assert that the organization of the American landscape represented "an aesthetic process that has scarcely been touched," this is decidedly less true for England, where the landscape has been subject to continuous and ef-

fective organization at least since Enclosure (the redistribution of grazing and crop land and the creation of private estates from communal holdings) reached its peak in the seventeenth and eighteenth centuries. Even now, England is far more subject than the United States to rigorous zoning, which regulates every aspect of land use. In addition, it is a nation fairly groaning under the burden of industrial development. In such a land, there is less occasion and less tolerance for the large-scale interventions of an art sometimes wilfully unbeautiful.

While still a student in 1967 Long had made ephemeral sculptures in the landscape: concentric circles of paper laid on the ground or paths trodden in the grass. On a rocky Somerset beach in 1968 he arranged a group of stones in the barely perceptible outline of a square. And in 1969 he made walking itself

34

33. Richard Long (b. 1945). *Walking a Line in Peru*, 1972. Photograph by the artist.

34. Richard Long. *A Line in Bolivia*, 1981. Photograph by the artist.

35. Richard Long. *A Line in the Himalayas*, 1975. Photograph by the artist.

36. Richard Long. *A Line in Scotland, Cul Mór*, 1981. Photograph by the artist.

into a sculpture: from the twelfth to the fifteenth of October, for example, Long walked the figures of four concentric squares in the Wiltshire countryside. Each square was walked as accurately as possible, the time noted and the square drawn on a map. The activity constituted the artwork; the map provided its visual record.

"A walk is on the ground, passing by, moving through life. A sculpture is still; a stopping place."[37] Thus Long in 1981 described the distinction between his two forms of art making. A photographic work from 1973 serves as an emblem of this distinction. It consists of ten black and white images of irregular but roughly circular groupings of stones in the landscape. As Long walked, he paused at intervals to rearrange the stones he encountered along the way, and then photographed them. The group of photographs he entitled *A Rolling Stone. Resting Places along a Journey, 1973*. He used stones as his medium. ("Stones are the material of the Earth. I pray the Earth still has a future.") Long himself can be seen as the rolling stone; the sculptures are the discreet signs of his resting places.

By now it seems that Long has walked nearly everywhere: in the Himalayas and the Andes, on Dartmoor and in Africa. Sometimes he simply walks, and records his journeys on a map. At other times, he has continued to make his unobtrusive marks in the landscape: not just with stones, but with driftwood and seaweed and bits of shrubbery as well. His preference is for the more remote and uninhabited, even exotic landscapes; there is a melancholy absence of any human trace except his own in his photographs. The configuration of his walks and the form of his marks have remained unwaveringly simple: circles and squares, spirals and straight lines. These are simple shapes with multiple references. "A circle is shared, common knowledge. It belongs equally to the past, the present and the future." The circle, the line, and

the spiral are employed precisely because of these associations; Long appropriates them to render his privately ritualistic work more universal. Sometimes these appropriations are quite literal. *Walking a Line in Peru, 1972* took place on one of the extraordinary ground markings made over two thousand years ago by the Nazca Indians on the coastal deserts of Peru. In 1975 Long walked every road, lane, and double track within a six-mile radius of the Cerne Abbas Giant, an ithyphallic chalk drawing on a hillside in Dorset. His lines have also traced the course of recent history. *Power Line Walk: From a Water Wheel to a Nuclear Power Station* in 1980 emphasized the relentless and potentially cataclysmic development of technology. "A walk is just one more layer, a mark," Long explains, "laid upon the thousands of other layers of human and geographic history on the surface of the land."[38]

As Smithson did with his Nonsites, Long sometimes brings his sculptures indoors to galleries or museums. No doubt he feels a measure of frustration in this, for these works can never match the layered, richly referential quality of the works in the landscape. Yet they too are signifiers of Long's resolute involvement with earth and its materials. Some of these sculptures are simple circles or rectangles of indigenous materials; others recreate the distance of outdoor walks. For the Whitechapel Art Gallery in London in 1971, Long compressed a line the length of a straight walk from the bottom to the top of Silbury Hill — a large, man-made mound in Wiltshire — into a spiral that fit within the walls of the gallery. The indoor line itself was made by walking: Long coated his feet with clay and imprinted the piece on the floor.

Long expresses through his work only an implied comment on the more interventionist projects of his American contemporaries. Hamish Fulton is more explicit. Asked in a recent interview how he regarded

35

36

37. Richard Long. *California Wood Circle*,
1976. Wood; diameter: 18 ft. Musée de l'Art
Moderne, Centre Georges Pompidou, Paris.

38. Hamish Fulton (b. 1946). *Standing Coyote*,
1981. Photograph by the artist.

39. Hamish Fulton. *Ringdom Gompa*, 1978.
Photograph by the artist.

37

Smithson, Heizer, and De Maria, Fulton replied that he believed artists ought to support each other, but went on to say, "I feel the three artists you mention use the landscape without . . . any sense of respect for it. . . . I see their art as a continuation of 'Manifest Destiny'. . . the so-called 'heroic conquering' of nature."[39] Acknowledging that they generally work outside the city, he said that he nevertheless found the content of their work to be "inescapably urban." To the extent that rapture before nature has always been felt most strongly by those most alienated from it—i.e., inhabitants of a large city—Fulton is certainly correct. But his work is equally reactionist; in this sense it too is urban generated. "My art is a passive protest against urban societies that alienate people from the world of nature."[40]

The walk is also Fulton's principal form of activity. But, unlike Long, the walk itself is not his artwork. "The walk is the walk and the artwork is the framed photograph and text,"

he explained. Somewhere along the way, he makes a photograph that evokes either the landscape he has passed through or his state of mind. Fulton also differs from Long in that he never makes a mark of any sort — other than footprints — in the landscape. He is the most emphatically reverential of these artists. "The natural environment was not built by man and for this reason it is to me deeply mysterious and religious."[41] Consequently, he does not alter it, and he prefers to select landscapes with little or no evidence of human activity. "The photographs show the land the way it should remain." People generally do not appear in Fulton's work, except, for example, in a few photographs taken in the Himalayas or the rural areas of Bolivia, where he feels people live in greater harmony with the natural environment.

David Nash has entwined his art-making and his existence even more resolutely. If Long and Fulton demonstrate how personal behavior or ritual can become art, then Nash

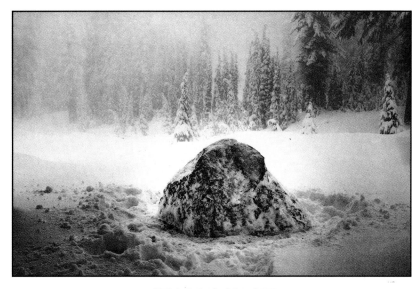

STANDING COYOTE

A SEVEN DAY WALK IN NORTHEASTERN CALIFORNIA

ENDING ON THE NIGHT OF THE OCTOBER FULL MOON 1981

RINGDOM GOMPA

NORTHERN INDIA   JULY 1978

A 14½ DAY WALKING JOURNEY OF APPROXIMATELY 200 MILES TRAVELLING BY WAY OF

RINGDOM GOMPA   THE PEN ZI PASS   THE ZANSKAR RIVER   ATING GOMPA

HUTTRA   THE MUNI GLACIER   MACHAIL AND THE CHANDER BHAGA RIVER

40. David Nash (b. 1945). *Chorus Line (Three Dandy Scuttlers)*, 1976. Oak and beech: height: 63 in. Private collection.

reveals how the practice of art can become a way of life. After he completed art college in London in 1967, Nash removed himself to one of Britain's wettest mountain fastnesses, the slate-quarrying village of Blaenau Ffestiniog in North Wales. One can hardly imagine a less picturesque place: Nash described it as "a small derelict quarrying town, just above the tree line."[42] It is surrounded by slag tips that rival the mountains in height; on the many rainy days, sky and slag coalesce in a somber and monochrome gray. Nash maintains that it was pragmatism, at least in part, that led him to Blaenau. Life is far less expensive there than in London; he was able to acquire a large chapel in which to work, with living quarters behind it. But Nash was also motivated by dissatisfaction with the stranglehold of the urban centers on contemporary art, an attitude that was shared by many in England and America at the time. A single encounter with Blaenau was enough to convince me that Nash was obviously not in search of an arcadian alternative. He selected an unbeautiful village, where he lives in close proximity to his neighbors in an emphatically Welsh community that the more fainthearted might find alarmingly parochial.

It was here that Nash began to work with wood. At first, it was milled lumber, but soon it was wood from trees that he cut himself. "Three valleys fall away from this damp grey ledge toward the sea. In the valleys are trees." Green wood and dead; ash, oak, and beech: they were axed and sawed into balls, roped together into tripods and arches, or fashioned into tables with stacks of rough circles and blocks upon them. These were deliberately coarse pieces, without the finished look of fine carpentry. The green wood cracked as it seasoned; the surfaces were irregular, and pegs protruded from the joins.

In 1977 Nash added planted pieces to his sculptural repertory. Twenty-two ash trees were planted in a thirty-foot circle on land he

40

owns near Blaenau. Over a period of thirty years, they will be thrice fletched — cut part way through and bent over — and thereby coaxed to grow into an *Ash Dome*, which Nash expects to resemble "a volcano of growing energy." This was an idea locally inspired; hedgerows used for fencing are often made by such fletching. It also has considerable artistic precedent: elaborate topiary chambers were a feature in medieval gardens, while Alexander Pope apparently suggested to the poet William Shenstone that Shenstone plant on his ornamented farm, The Leasowes, a stand of trees that would grow to resemble a Gothic cathedral.[43] Two other pieces were planted by Nash in 1978 in Grizedale Forest, near the Lake District in Cumbria. One was a ring of larch trees, planted on the diagonal to

44

46

41. David Nash. *Wooden Waterway, Kakehi*, 1982. Mizunara (water oak), stone, and water; length: 100 ft. Collection of the Tochigi Prefectural Museum of Fine Arts, Japan.

42. David Nash. *Wooden Waterway*, 1978. Oak, ash, sycamore, birch, stone, and water; length: 150 ft. Grizedale Forest, Cumbria, England.

give them the appearance of sweeping down a slope. The other was a *Willow Ladder*, for which two young willow trees were cut down and inverted in the soil. Willows will root quite willingly from any point on the trunk or branches: these upside-down trees will sprout from their trunk tops shoots that will be entwined to form a structure like a ladder.

At the same time, Nash has continued with his cut pieces. He gouged troughs in fallen tree trunks and laid them end to end, beginning in a small spring and running down a hill, forming a wooden waterway with forks and falls. He quartered a tree trunk, each part of which had a branch, and pegged the parts together to form a *Running Table*: a great lumbering beast in the forest. Nash plants and cuts; he works with living wood and dead. He has come to identify with wood as a metaphor for his own life. "I want a simple approach to living and doing. I want a life and work that reflects the balance and continuity of nature. Identifying with the time and energy of the tree and with its mortality, I find myself drawn deeper into the joys and blows of nature. Worn down and regenerated; broken off and reunited; a dormant faith revived in the new growth on old wood."[44]

If there is something self-conscious in Nash's close identification of his art and his life, it is amply excused by the quality of his work, which has become more simple and more deft as he matures. He allows the wood to retain its own character, while not being reluctant to coax from it biomorphic forms. In this, he is in the tradition of Henry Moore and Barbara Hepworth, the great British practitioners of an abstracted but still organically suggestive naturalism. At the same time, he is not afraid of a certain amount of whimsical surrealism and the touch of modesty that it brings to his sculpture. The bestial character of the Grizedale *Running Table* has already been noted; it is also evident in the amusing *Chorus Line (Three Dandy Scuttlers)*.

41

42

43. David Nash. *Running Table*, 1978. Oak; height: 60 in. Grizedale Forest, Cumbria, England.

44. David Nash. *Fletched Over Ash Dome*, 1977. Pencil, charcoal, and watercolor on paper; 29¼ x 41¼ in. Private collection.

45. David Nash. *Wooden Fish*, 1982. Mizunara (water oak). Collection of the Tochigi Prefectural Museum of Fine Arts, Japan.

43

Fletched over Ash Dome

Planted March 1977 at Caen-y-Coed, Maentwrog, North Wales.

22 young ash trees planted in a circle (March 1977)

5 year old ash.   10 year old.   15 years old.   18 years old.   27 years old.

Planted on a promontory on a hillside.
By tending, grafting and fletching the trees
will be persuaded into a 30ft Dome.
Three 'Fletches' at ten year intervals.
Once the Dome is formed there will be no
further pruning or tending.

The Ash Dome
A silver linear structure in winter,
a green mass in summer,
a Volcano of growing energy.

David Nash

44

45

As Nash's reputation has grown, he has been invited to work farther and farther away from Blaenau: in the United States, Holland, and Japan. While this distance from his home base might be expected to weaken his work, it has not. In Japan, in particular, Nash and his hosts felt what can only be described as a remarkable sense of mutual self-recognition. For the exhibition *Aspects of British Art Today*, which opened in Tokyo and toured Japan in 1982, arrangements were made for Nash to go to Japan and work in a rural, mountainous area above Nikko, where an aged mizunara, or water oak tree, was found for him. He spent twenty days there, fashioning from the 45 tree some ten pieces, including *Wooden Fish, Cracking Box*, an arch, a wood stove, a wooden waterway (later permanently installed at the Tochigi Prefectural Museum of Fine Arts), and *River Tunnel*, a hollow log that was set adrift with a fire burning inside it. Nash's sensitivity to the biomorphically suggestive forms inherent in wood—what might be termed a reverence for the spirit of the material—drew comment from the Japanese for its relationship to Shinto, the pre-Buddhist veneration of nature spirits. To Nash, different trees have distinctive characters, "an oak being defined as brutal and full of compact energy, while a birch is seen as delicate, ethereal and passive."[45] *Wooden Fish* certainly exploited both the form and spirit inherent in the wood; it had the additional appeal of an oblique reference to the architecture of Japanese temples with their multiple, upturned, and overhanging cornices.

Nash's natural gregariousness has made him something of a patron of recent landscape art in Britain. Students come to live and work with him, and he encourages younger artists with whom he feels a kinship. One such is Andy Goldsworthy, who lives in Cumbria. Goldsworthy has spent some time in 46 Blaenau, making while there a large slate arch that resembled the bridges spanning the creeks on the upland moors. But Goldsworthy is a wanderer in the spirit of Long and Fulton, and creates his subtle and mysterious works as he goes. He gathers sticks and weaves them into spheres. In a patch of leaves on the ground he cuts an opening 48 through the green leaves on top, exposing the rotted ones below and creating a dark circle of decay. He gathers heron or crow feath- 49 ers, splitting them open to make a jagged line drawing on the earth. He combines these feathers with autumnal leaves to make brilliantly colored collages that are dispersed by the first wind. Goldsworthy preserves these private oblations in exquisite photographs. He is one of the very few of the recent artists in the landscape to make a virtue of fine photography. While most others feel that photographic refinement obscures the true, nonphotographic content of their work, Goldsworthy rightly finds it necessary for conveying the immaculacy of his efforts.

Although the ramble seems a particularly British approach to the landscape, it is an American who has developed wandering into a true epic. That the work of Charles Simonds should be described as epic might come as a surprise, given its diminuitive scale. But each piece he makes is an episode in an extended narrative, told in a consistent voice and celebrating the sweeping history of an imaginary civilization of little people. That Simonds figures in a discussion of contemporary art and landscape might also seem odd given the frequently urban and sometimes indoor settings of his work. Yet implicit in his art is a constant and almost mystical sense of earth as the giver of all life. The little people demonstrate an indissoluble bond with the physical and spiritual constituents of their environment. Simonds is their chronicler and their cultural geographer, telling their history and revealing how they live in different landscapes (and, by implication, how we live in ours). If Sim-

46. Andy Goldsworthy (b. 1956). *Arch*, 1982.
Stone. Blaenau Ffestiniog, Wales. Photograph
by the artist.

47. Andy Goldsworthy. *Cracked/Broken Pebbles*, 1978. Lancashire, England. Photograph by the artist.

48. Andy Goldsworthy. *Elder Patch*, 1983. Brough, Cumbria, England. Photograph by the artist.

49. Andy Goldsworthy. *Heron Feathers*, March 1982. Photograph by the artist.

50. Andy Goldsworthy. *Stacked Sticks*, June 1980. Photograph by the artist.

47

48

49

50

51. Andy Goldsworthy. *Tossing Sticks in the Air*, July 10, 1980. Cumbria, England. Photograph by the artist.

51

52. Charles Simonds (b. 1945). *Dwelling, P.S. 1, Long Island City, New York*, 1975. Clay and wood; length of bricks: ½ in. Temporary installation. Collection of the artist.

onds's presence is not often seen in the physical landscape, it is still to be felt in the landscape of fantasy and the intellect.

Simonds gave symbolic birth to himself and to the little people in a New Jersey clay pit in 1970, where he had himself filmed emerging naked from the muck. Like Adam, he was clay made animate; he was simultaneously exploiting the sexual and sacred associations of earth. Later, covered again with clay, he lay down, making himself into a landscape. On the hillside of his hip, he constructed the dwellings of the little people. This ritual, called *Landscape ↔ Body ↔ Dwelling*, asserted his own sense of identity with the earth and the link between the architectural forms of the little people and the physical character of their environment. The earth, architecture, and the body were analogized as different forms of dwellings.

Since the enactment of the birth ritual, Simonds and his miniature civilization have been all around the world: to Paris, Genoa, Berlin, even Shanghai. He began by building their dwellings on abandoned buildings and in vacant lots on the Lower East Side of New York. He was all the time elaborating the fantasy of their migrations, appropriate to that decaying quarter of New York that has been home to successive waves of immigrants. He worked by spreading clay on a ledge or in a niche, then building with tiny clay bricks the shelters and ritual places of his little people. Dwellings were clustered on slopes or made to surround domed kivas; altars were built on breast and genital shapes that occurred in the landscape. Labyrinths, tombs, observatories, and arenas of justice were formed to allude to the work habits and beliefs of this civilization. As the art world began to take notice, museums and private collectors throughout the United States and Europe commissioned his works. The little people were presented for themselves, but also as a tool for examining our own architecture and social struc-

tures. Each piece offered a comparison: between the technologically naive little people —whose architecture conformed to the contours of the landscape and whose earth-centered rituals were everywhere in evidence —and the technologically sophisticated constructions of our urban environments, imposed upon if not hostile to the landscape.

The history of the little people is told primarily through Simonds's sculptures. He has provided them with one eloquent written account, however, which reveals that they wander as freely as their creator. Entitled *Three Peoples*, this small book tells of three branches of the miniature civilization: the linear, circular, and spiral peoples.[46] The linear people inched along through the landscape, building new homes adjacent to their last ones, leaving all their possessions behind when they moved as a museum of personal artifacts. "Their dwellings make a pattern on the earth as of a great tree laid flat, branching and forking according to their loves and hates, forming an ancestral record of life lived as an odyssey, its roots in a dark and distant past. . . ." The circular people bridged the past and the future. They were careful historians, marking time and recording the past, but their life's energies were concentrated on a yearly ritual of procreation that "reenacted original creation in a dizzying celebration of sexual possibility." The circular people lived within a closed system, moving always within the same circle. They built their new dwellings on the remains of the old, advancing one unit each year away from the recent past and into the distant past. At the center of the circle was the underground kiva, the "dome-womb" that was the site of the orgiastic dance on the winter solstice.

The spiral people yearned only for an ecstatic death. They built their dwellings in an ascending ring that tightened upon itself, "with the past, constantly buried, serving as a building material for the future." They cared little for their surroundings or their relationship to the natural environment. They built their dwellings higher and higher, throwing their artifacts and, as the living space was reduced, even themselves into the center of the spiral to support its climb. Their sacrifice was volitional: "They believed resolutely that they were contributing to the most ambitious monument ever conceived by man." Their goal "was to achieve both the greatest possible height and to predict the very moment of collapse, the moment when the last of their resources would be consumed and their death inevitable. They lived for that moment alone." There is more than a coincidental similarity between the spiral people and ourselves. They are Simonds's evocation of twentieth-century man.

As the omniscient chronicler of the little people's history, Simonds bears an intriguing resemblance to characterizations of the Wandering Jew, that eternal traveler who has lived the entire history of his people since the Crucifixion. Condemned to wander endlessly for his denial of Christ on the road to Calvary, the Wandering Jew achieves in many versions of the story — particularly that of Guillaume Apollinaire[47] — an almost godly knowledge of life. He is a tireless observer of events who has been everywhere and seen everything. He is set apart by his profound knowledge. As Simonds's little people are a race of wanderers, so is he their Wandering Jew, their historian and cultural geographer. A sense of his own peregrinations informs the work: an

early exposure to the cliff dwellings and kivas of the Southwestern American Indians provided him with a basic vocabulary of forms, which was elaborated by subsequent study of other prehistoric civilizations as well as animal architecture and botanical shapes. His wanderings have also led to an awareness of and a commentary on present-day social and environmental conditions. Using the forms and myths of the little people, he has participated in the development of inner-city parks and playlots; proposed the creation of hanging gardens in abandoned tenements; and constructed a human-scaled circular dwelling of earth and seeds that was converted from shelter to food as the plants matured.

Simonds and his British contemporaries share a kind of preindustrial innocence. Combined with their modesty in scale is a freedom from the tools and techniques required by the more grandiose projects of the Americans. Like latter-day Luddites — those British working men who, at the turn of the nineteenth century, smashed the newly created textile machinery that threatened their employment — these artists recoil from the perceived malevolence of many modern developments. Not all are as explicit as Long, with his earnest plea, "I pray the Earth still has a future." But taken together these artists express a conscious and articulate reaction to our alarming capacity to lay waste to our landscapes and dwellings through a technological capability that seems to exceed the limits of our wisdom and sanity.

57

53

54

55

56

53. Charles Simonds. *Landscape ↔ Body ↔ Dwelling*, 1973. Clay; length of bricks: ½ in. Collection of the artist.

54. Charles Simonds. *Picaresque Landscape*, 1976, detail of linear and circular dwellings. Clay, wood, and plaster; 16 x 19 ft. Temporary installation at the Museum of Modern Art, New York. Collection of the artist.

55. Charles Simonds. *Age*, 1982–83, detail. Clay, wood, and plaster; height: 10 ft., diameter: 30 ft. Temporary installation at the Solomon R. Guggenheim Museum, New York. Courtesy of Castelli Feigen Corcoran Gallery.

56. Charles Simonds. *Dwelling, Chicago*, 1981, detail. Clay and wood; overall length: 44 ft. Permanent installation at the Museum of Contemporary Art, Chicago, Illinois.

57. Charles Simonds. *Growth House*, 1975. Ink on paper; 25 x 29½ in. Collection of the artist. This is a seasonably renewable dwelling. As the seeds sprout, growth transforms the built structure; the dwelling is transformed from shelter to food and harvested and eaten.

57

58. This is a general view of the Garden of History at Pratt Farm, near Clinton, Maine, which was begun by James Pierce in 1970. The *Turf Maze* and its *Observatory* can be seen in the foreground; *Earthwoman* appears in the distance.

3. TRADITION AND ANTECEDENT

Art in the landscape encompasses multiple allusions, some of which have been touched upon already. The technological innocence shared by Simonds and some of his British and American contemporaries, together with an earnest longing for the kind of close accord with the natural world we assume to be characteristic of earlier peoples, provide a link to the culture of prehistory. This link is also asserted through the use of archaisms (as discussed in chapter 1): the solstitial alignments of both Holt's *Sun Tunnels* and Morris's *Observatory*, for example, or the mastaba shape of Heizer's *Complex One*. The significance of this correspondence with prehistoric art lies in its implied refutation of mainstream contemporary culture, with its emphasis on consumption and conformity to fashion. By reviving an anonymous tradition of earthworking as a form of artistic activity and by removing themselves to distant locations land artists hoped, however quixotically, to free themselves from these unpleasant associations. They were continuing a tendency in modern art identified by Robert Goldwater in 1938 as "Romantic Primitivism": the use of models from outside the tradition of Western European art, such as African or Oceanic sculpture, to reinvigorate the forms and purposes of the prevailing art.[48]

Goldwater also identified a concern for the purity of abstract form as an expression of "Intellectual Primitivism." Freed from realism's limitations of representation and narration, abstract works were felt by many in this century to be more capable of conveying to the viewer universal, basic, and eternal sensations. This was certainly true of several of the Abstract Expressionist painters. "Abstraction enables man to break the finite barrier and enter into the actuality of infinity," Arshile Gorky wrote.[49] And Barnett Newman asserted that Theodoros Stamos "reveals an attitude toward nature that is closer to true communion. . . . He redefines the pastoral experience as one of participation with the inner life of the natural phenomenon. . . . In this Stamos is on the same fundamental ground as the primitive artist who never portrayed the phenomenon as an object of romance and sentiment, but always as an expression of the original noumenistic mystery in which rock and man are equal."[50] The abstract image — whether in primitive or modern art—was felt to present reality as known in the mind rather than merely perceived by the senses. It became a visible icon for the metaphysical. Adolph Gottlieb and Mark Rothko asserted that "the subject is crucial and only that subject matter is valid which is tragic and timeless. That is why we profess kinship with primitive and archaic art."[51] Their tragic and timeless subjects were also abstract.

In their use of reductive forms to convey metaphysical content, several of the land artists—Heizer and De Maria chief among them — share in this intellectual primitivism. But their work can also be interpreted as a contemporary expression of the sublime. Indeed, the evocations of this eighteenth-century aesthetic and philosophical attitude toward the landscape are no less pervasive than the allusions to prehistory; they are merely less frequently discussed. The sublime has figured in considerations of Abstract Expressionist painting,[52] but its applicability to land art is equally intriguing. The eighteenth century also produced an answer to the sublime in the theories of the picturesque, which were applied to painting and landscape design long before they were given extended written exposition. As suggested in the introduction, the picturesque literally transformed the British landscape and was conveyed to the United States most eloquently through the work of Olmsted and Vaux. It, too, continues to have a significant impact today.

Edmund Burke's *Philosophical Enquiry into the Origin of Our Ideas of the Sublime and Beautiful*, published in England in 1757, dif-

59

59, 60. Walter De Maria (b. 1935). *The Lightning Field*, 1974–77. Stainless steel poles; average height of poles: 20 ft. 7½ in.; overall dimensions: 5,280 x 3,300 ft. Near Quemado, New Mexico. Collection of the Dia Art Foundation.

ferentiated between two principal classes of objects and, by implication, of landscapes and vistas. Those that were smooth, gentle, and pleasing stimulated the instinct of self-propagation and were thus perceived as beautiful. Those that induced terror by a suggestion of solitude, vastness, or power touched the instinct of self-preservation and were perceived as sublime. Writing in 1927, the art historian Christopher Hussey attributed seven characteristics to the sublime, based on his reading of Burke: *obscurity*, both physical and intellectual; *power*; *privations*, such as darkness, solitude, and silence; *vastness*, either vertical or horizontal, both of which diminish the relative scale of the human observer; *infinity*, which could either be literal or induced by two final characteristics of the sublime: *succession* and *uniformity*, both of which suggest limitless progression.[53]

Hussey's seven attributes of the sublime provide a virtual prescription for Walter De Maria's *Lightning Field*, completed in 1977 near Quemado, New Mexico. De Maria's piece is composed of 400 stainless steel poles 2 inches in diameter, standing at an average height of 20 feet, 7½ inches, in such a way that all the tops are level. They are arranged in a grid with 16 rows of 25 poles stretching east to west and 25 rows of 16 poles stretching north to south. The poles are 225 feet apart, 311 on the diagonal, with the total east-west dimension of the piece running exactly one mile, the north-south distance just over a kilometer.

The Lightning Field stands in a flat, semi-arid basin in west-central New Mexico; the site is ringed by distant mountains. This is an area of seemingly limitless vistas and a numerically negligible human population. It is also a region with a relatively high incidence of lightning. For all these reasons, it was a location that particularly appealed to De Maria. He planned his work scrupulously to attract the lightning and thereby to celebrate its power and visual splendor. He wanted a place where one could be alone with a trackless earth and an overarching sky to witness their potent interchange through apparently wanton electrical discharge. The work is neither of the earth nor of the sky but is of both; it is the means to an epiphany for those viewers susceptible to an awesome natural phenomenon. Few leave *The Lightning Field* untouched by the splendid desolation of its setting and the majesty of its purpose.

But few are lucky enough actually to witness lightning discharging itself on De Maria's rods. For all other visitors, *The Lightning Field* has more subtle charms. It is a fugitive work, disappearing in the bright midday sun and becoming visible only at dawn and dusk when the entire length of each pole glows with reflected light. At all times the piece is an experience in the demarcation of space, referring through the use of the mile and the kilometer to the manner in which much of the earth has been divided and brought under human sovereignty. The grid form and the mile dimension in particular bring to mind the endless mile-square sections that form a checkerboard across the Midwest and West, which resulted from Jefferson's National Survey of 1785. Like De Maria's *Las Vegas Piece*, *The Lightning Field* is also an experience of the relatively insignificant physical scale of humans and their creations when contrasted to the vast basins and ranges that compose the geography of the American Southwest.

It is probable that De Maria intended to evoke the sublime; yet it seems unlikely that he was aware of how exactly he employed its attributes as defined by Hussey. His *Lightning Field* is *obscure*, both in the sense of being difficult to perceive — especially at midday — and in being remote and troublesome to reach. Its central image is *power* — the sometimes lethal power of lightning.

The *privations* of solitude and silence are integral to the experience of the work; it is *vast*, both in its own dimension and in the setting it employs. And everywhere is the inference of *infinity*. The poles stand in stately *succession*, *uniform* in height and in the distance between them. As they diminish in the distance, they create the illusion — like telephone poles or railroad tracks — of endless progression. This is reinforced by a tidy and clever mathematical sequence: the number of poles on the kilometer side is equivalent to four-squared; on the mile side five-squared; the total number of poles is twenty-squared. One can extrapolate an endless grid from this numerical formula. The infinite is also in evidence, if not in the horizontal spread of the earth, then in the extraterrestrial dominions to which the work emphatically points.

Other works compare to De Maria's in effect. The grand scale and emptiness of the Western landscape perhaps make an association with the sublime unavoidable for any art work created there. But the selection of sites often remote and uninhabited emphasizes its characteristics, as does the use of simple, commanding forms. By excavating a space for his *Double Negative*, Heizer literally wraps one in solitude. By focusing one's view through her *Sun Tunnels*, Holt emphasizes the discomfiture produced by a sense of great distance. And the projected works of Turrell and Ross both may have the result of underscoring the puniness and mortality of humanity in comparison with the infinite scale and duration of the heavens.

In his *Essay on the Picturesque* (1794), the Englishman Uvedale Price added a third category of objects—and landscapes—to Burke's beautiful and sublime ones. Price felt that the sublime and the beautiful failed to account for those things that were crude, rustic, and irregular, but visually engaging nevertheless. These he described as *picturesque*; literally, like a picture, especially those of Jan van Goyen, Jacob van Ruisdael, Salvator Rosa, and Claude Lorrain. To Price, the landscape paintings of these men, with their sudden and extreme contrasts of light and dark, their intricate and irregular compositions and oftentimes rustic or humble subjects, represented just those qualities that were neither sublime nor beautiful, but found expression in the picturesque.

Another English essayist, Richard Payne Knight, simultaneously offered a competing view of the picturesque in *The Landscape: A Didactic Poem*, 1794; and *Analytical Inquiry into the Principles of Taste*, 1805. Although Knight agreed with Price that it was largely aesthetic or objective qualities that produced a picturesque effect, he suggested that there were nonaesthetic elements that contributed as well. These elements functioned psychologically, arousing multiple ideas and associations. This principle of association had its relevance to painting and landscape design alike. The appearance of a Gothic ruin, a Chinese temple, a Druidical stone circle, or even a hermit's cottage enhanced a picturesque effect by evoking the ancient, the unfamiliar, or the exotic.

While the principles of the picturesque were not codified until late in the eighteenth century, they had begun to find expression some eighty years before in early Georgian garden design. The visual values of complexity, irregularity, and concealment began to be favored over geometrical plans; while some formality remained, variety and a sensitivity to the vagaries of natural terrain became the mode of the day. Charles Bridgeman and William Kent were the most prominent practitioners of this new aesthetic in the first half of the century. Horace Walpole, Joseph Addison, and Alexander Pope were among those who provided the written foundations for the landscape attitudes that were later modified and elaborated into the picturesque by William Gilpin, Price, and Knight.[54]

61. Begun in the mid-eighteenth century by Henry Hoare, Stourhead is one of the best preserved of the picturesque landscape parks in Britain.

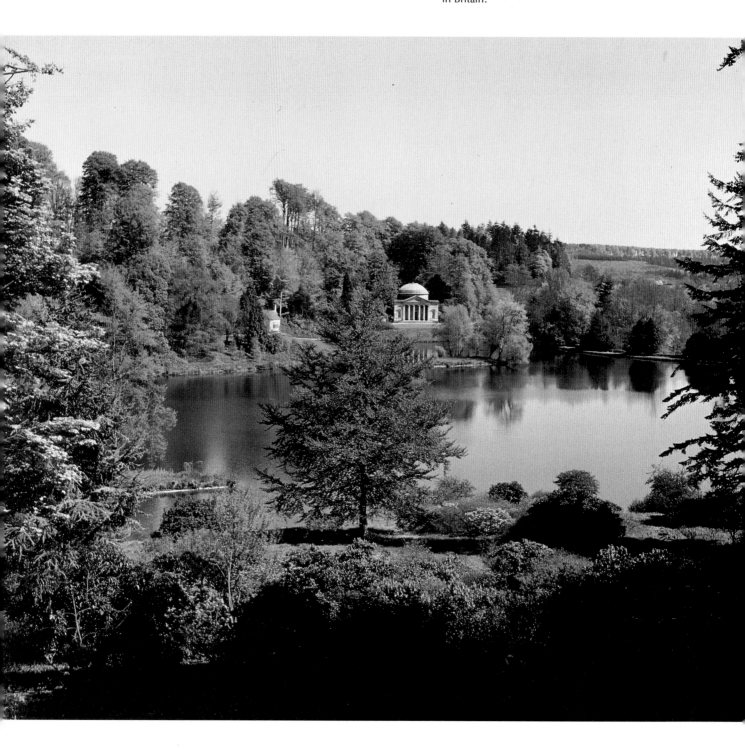

Bridgeman and Kent both worked at Stowe in Buckinghamshire, perhaps the most widely known of the early eighteenth-century landscaped parks; Pope created his own celebrated but long since destroyed garden at Twickenham.

But it was a banker and amateur gardener, Henry Hoare, who gave us what is one of the best preserved of the landscapes arranged in the picturesque manner. Begun at mid-century, Stourhead includes both open meadows and dense groupings of trees, an irregularly shaped artificial lake, hills, fine prospects, and shadowed vales that obscure all views. A pathway meanders through the landscape, around the lake, past streams and cascades. Stourhead also incorporates associative elements, sometimes known as follies. These diverse structures — a stone grotto with statues of a river god and a nymph, Temples of Apollo and Flora, a rustic cottage and convent, a Pantheon, an obelisk — add to the visual variety of the park, and enhance the picturesque effect by evoking unfamiliar cultures or ancient civilizations.

The visual and psychological complexity thus achieved is underscored by a rich and apparently autobiographical iconographic program.[55] Over the entrance to the grotto is an inscription from Book I of the *Aeneid*; another from Book II is in the Temple of Flora. The circuit walk around the lake may have been intended as an allegory of Aeneas's travels, with particular reference to his descent into the underworld to see his father, which began at Lake Avernus. Hoare's only son had died in 1751, so he may have felt especially inspired to evoke this story of the reunion of father and son, above and beyond the then customary appreciation for classical literature.

The picturesque finds its strongest contemporary expression in the work of James Pierce at Pratt Farm on the Kennebec River in central Maine. Pierce combines the visual values of the picturesque with its associative or evocative elements. He has created over the last dozen years on seventeen acres of meadow and woodland a work he describes as a "garden of history," that is, a landscaped park containing numerous individual but interdependent elements rich with historical associations. He began in the summer of 1970 with the excavation of a still unfinished *Kiva*, based on the Indian ceremonial structures also evoked by Simonds. The next summer and every summer since, Pierce has added to his garden of history. First came a pair of forts and a burial mound. The *Triangular* and *Circular Redoubts* are made of mounded turf and are similar to crude fortifications used in North America by the British and French in the eighteenth century; indeed, Pierce sometimes calls these the *British* and *French Redoubts* in observance of the fact that for a time the Kennebec marked the boundary between the colonial settlements of these two nations. The *Burial Mound*, like the *Kiva*, is modeled on Indian prototypes and is intended eventually to hold the remains of its creator.

Between 1972 and 1974, Pierce executed an unusual triangular *Turf Maze* some 120 feet on a side. Although based on the plan of a topiary maze published in the seventeenth century, it is formed of earth in the manner of late medieval models, like Richard Fleischner's contemporaneous *Sod Maze*. But unlike Fleischner's work, it is cut into the ground with raised pathways between the cuts, and the path to the center is not continuous, but confounding, marked by choices and dead ends. A small *Observatory* provides an overlook for the *Maze*. On a hill above it, Pierce built in 1975 a spiral hill, or *Motte*, eight feet high and twenty feet in diameter. Like the *Redoubts*, it brings to mind defensive structures, in this case the mounts that sometimes form the central keep in medieval castles.

62. James Pierce (b. 1930). *Triangular Redoubt*, 1971. Earth; height: 5 ft., length of each side: 65 ft. Pratt Farm.

63. James Pierce. *Stone Ship*, 1975. 40 ft. x 12 ft. *Burial Mound*, 1971. Earth; height: 4 ft., diameter: 4 ft. Pratt Farm.

64. James Pierce. *Altar*, 1977. Wood and rock; 7½ ft. x 23 in. x 12 in. Pratt Farm.

62

63

64

Several more burial monuments were added to Pratt Farm in the mid-1970s. Near the *Burial Mound*, Pierce arrayed a group of glacial boulders to suggest the partially disrupted outlines of a boat, which rises in profile toward the bow and stern. This *Stone Ship* alludes to Viking burial practices: the deceased were sometimes interred in their boats. At forty feet long and twelve feet wide, it is approximately the size of the precariously small Viking vessels that explored the northeast coast of North America a millennium ago. It is oriented to Polaris, in reference to both navigation and the voyage to the afterlife.

In a nearby grove of pine and birch trees, Pierce built another type of Scandinavian bronze-age tomb. This is the *Tree Burial*: a log large enough to contain a corpse that rests on a bed of glacial boulders. In an authentic burial, the log would have been hollowed out to contain the corpse. Near it is the *Shaman's Tomb*, a wooden coffin raised on four posts. It alludes to the belief among certain Siberian peoples that the soul of the deceased shaman was a bird that would return to the same family only if the body were left unburied.

Another piece of Central Asian inspiration stands in the woods near the *Tree Burial* and the *Shaman's Tomb*. This is a cruciform *Altar*, a single post and a crosspiece that supports two granite boulders. The iconography here is clearly Christian and amusingly sexual (as Pierce tells it, granite is igneous, a "hot rock"). But the altar also makes reference to the worship of stones among a Central Asian people, the Buriats, who, for the sake of agricultural fruitfulness, elevated on platforms certain stones that they believed had fallen from the sky.

The shift inaugurated by the *Altar* from mortuary to suggestively procreative works was continued in a group created between 1976 and 1978 in the central area of the garden. Under a large white pine that Pierce has designated the Tree of Life, he set a wooden ithyphallic *Monk's Post*. Near it is the recumbent *Earthwoman*, inspired by the dorsal view of the prehistoric Venus of Willendorf in Vienna. Some thirty feet long, half as wide, and five feet high, she lies face down, spread-eagled. She is oriented to the sunrise on the summer solstice, in such a way that the sun rises through the cleft in her buttocks in a symbolic fertilization. On the opposite side of the *Monk's Post* from her lies, face up, the similarly spread-eagled *Suntreeman*. Like the Cerne Abbas Giant in Dorset, he has an erect phallus. His arms suggest tree branches, and his round head, which doubles as a fire pit, alludes to the sun.

In 1979 Pierce coiled a *Stone Serpent* some eighty feet in length along the edge of the woods near the *Earthwoman*. At the same time, he continued with a number of earthen pieces. One was cut into the ground like the *Maze*: a schematic representation of a boat called the *Quebec Expedition*, commemorating Benedict Arnold's arduous passage in the autumn of 1775 up the Kennebec, past the site of Pratt Farm, on the way to his unsuccessful siege of British-held Quebec City. Another, the *Erechwagon*, was mounded like the *Sun-*

65

66

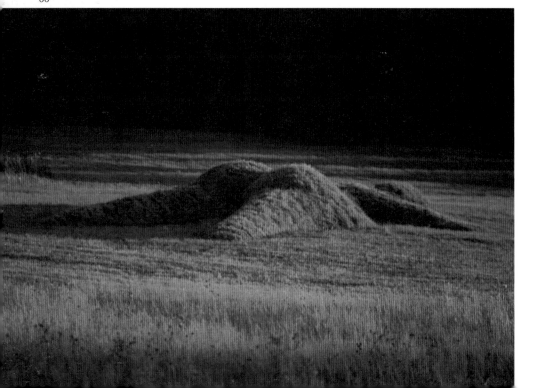

65. James Pierce. *Earthwoman*, 1976–77. Earth;
5 x 30 x 15 ft. View with a long grass coat.
Pratt Farm.

66. James Pierce. *Earthwoman*, view at sunset.

67. James Pierce. *Earthwoman*, sunrise on the
summer solstice.

67

68. James Pierce. *Suntreeman*, 1978. Earth and rock; 2 x 50 x 45 ft. Pratt Farm.

69. James Pierce. *Serpent*, 1979. Rock; 1 x 80 x 55 ft. Pratt Farm.

treeman and is based on the first known representation of a wheeled vehicle, found on a tablet about 5,500 years old at Erech, in present-day Iraq. The third is a four-faced Janus figure, a pyramidal mound with a profiled nose at each corner and eyes formed of ceramic pipes. Through one of the eyes of this *Janus*, symbol of ending and beginning, is visible the *Kiva*, the first work in Pierce's garden of history and the source of the earth for the *Janus*.

In no instance is any of these various works a direct copy of its prototype. Some, like the *Shaman's Tomb* or the *Stone Ship*, are free adaptations from a specific source. In others, the *Suntreeman* for example, there is no clear precedent at all but an inventive use of historically suggestive forms instead. These are not reproductions but evocations, consistent with the eighteenth-century picturesque use of associative elements. Like the Temple of Apollo or the grotto at Stourhead, Pierce's works are allusions to exotic cultures, prehistoric monuments, or partially forgotten episodes in the history of our own nation. They have a rich visual and psychological character, summoning recall of the indistinctly known past.

Pierce's historical forms are arrayed in a landscape that is itself picturesque. Open meadows contrast with dense stands of evergreen and birch, which meet the meadows in a serpentine line. At the bottom of a slope, the Kennebec pursues its meandering

68

69

course; the view of the opposite bank is dominated by a chapel spire. A series of alignments draws the works together, as between the *Kiva* and the *Janus*; the *Motte*, the *Observatory*, and the apex of the *Earthwoman* form an alignment with the chapel across the Kennebec. Picturesque vistas are also employed: breaks in the trees frame certain of the works, while paths through the woods grant telescopic views of others.

The kind of programmatic unity that has been detected at Stourhead is also evident at Pratt Farm. Pierce's work began with a series of forts and burial monuments, making his garden a mock necropolis. In the midst of these came the *Turf Maze*, representative of passage and choice and psychologically a more neutral work. The more recent pieces are dominated by images of fertility and procreation and, with the *Janus* figure, of ending and beginning anew. Pierce's garden of history is thus also a garden of life, death, and regeneration.

Other thematic interpretations are possible. Pierce works only with materials found at the site: soil, glacial boulders, deposits of sand and clay, and driftwood from the Kennebec. His is thus also a garden of natural history. And with his deliberate evocation of previous landscaped parks, it is even a garden of the

history of gardens of history. Individual works carry multiple meanings as well. The *Turf Maze* is an allegory of choice; in one's journey into and out from it, it is also an allegory of insemination and birth. The *Altar* is a cross; it is an erect phallus. The *Suntreeman* combines images of male potency with botanical growth; it can also be seen as a male Daphne transforming himself into a tree to elude the ravishments of some female Apollo. The white pine that dominates the center of the garden is the tree of life in the procreative group that includes the *Suntreeman* and the *Earthwoman*; it becomes the tree of knowledge when the same works are interpreted as Adam and Eve with the *Stone Serpent*.

"Modern sculpture is *wilfully* ignorant," the Scotsman Ian Hamilton Finlay has declared.[56] One suspects that few of the artists in this volume would escape his opprobrium, with the possible exception of Pierce. For Pierce is Finlay's only rival in a deliberately wide-ranging deployment of historical references in the full knowledge of their aesthetic, moral, and political implications. If Pierce is distinguished as a sculptor, landscapist, and historian, then Finlay is all of these and aesthetic philosopher and botanist as well. Beside his ecumenical knowledge, most other artists must seem myopic at the least.

71

70

71

72

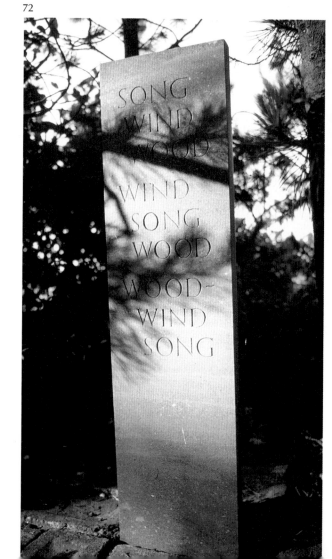

70. Ian Hamilton Finlay (b. 1925). *The Great Piece of Turf*, at Stonypath, begun 1967. Stone: 5 x 5 in., overall dimensions: 5 x 2 ft. Lanarks, Scotland.

71. Ian Hamilton Finlay. The main path in the front garden, Stonypath.

72. Ian Hamilton Finlay. *Wood Wind Song*. Slate stele in a grove of pines. Stonypath.

73. Ian Hamilton Finlay (with John Andrew). *Nuclear Sail*, c. 1973. Slate; height: 5 ft. Stonypath.

73

Even the most cursory exposure to Finlay's garden, Stonypath, in Lanarkshire in the southern regions of Scotland, suggests a veneration of the picturesque. Into a mere few acres is condensed a rich array of botanical specimens, sculpture, and poetic inscriptions. Finlay's garden is visually complex, incorporating ponds and streams and contrasting dense plantings with open grassy areas, the cultivated with the wild. Yet he does not aim for the appearance of nature untouched, which was the highest goal of the best known of the eighteenth-century landscape designers, Capability Brown. Instead, he aspires to an image of nature improved upon by the intellect. He writes that his garden "suggests the Neoplatonic idea of improved or Ideal Nature, as opposed to the modern view, which is of 'nature' itself as being the ideal (and more ideal the more it is untouched by the human intellect)."[57] In this he reveals a closer link to Nicolas Poussin, who organized his landscapes with precision and clarity to present nature as if it were perfect. Indeed, Finlay titled one of the exhibitions of his garden work *Nature Over Again After Poussin*,[58] an obvious play on Cézanne's avowal to do "Poussin over again after nature," but also and more importantly an exposition of the intellectual foundations for his work.

Finlay professes a kinship as well with the Neoclassicism of Jacques Louis David (himself a neo-Poussinist), with its deft combination of aesthetic and political content, and with the revolutionary ideology of David's contemporaries. As Neoclassicism was an assault on the corrupt and outmoded values of an absolutist regime, so is it Finlay's inspiration for his emphatic critique of the intellectual bankruptcy of contemporary culture. And as it was a recall of a presumably more learned age, so is it Finlay's means of entreaty for a more multidimensional world, for an end to what one of Finlay's principal enthusiasts has called "the vulgar disjunction of traditional culture and contemporary art."[59] "Tradition is not dead," Finlay writes, "it has never been heard of." Finlay quotes one of his heroes, the French revolutionary Louis Antoine Léon de Saint-Just: "the world has been empty since the Romans." One suspects that to Finlay, the world has likewise been empty since the philosopher-statesmen of the French Revolution dominated the politics and culture of their brief era. Finlay links Saint-Just with the notions of Jean Jacques Rousseau (another of his heroes) on the moral superiority of "natural man," describing Saint-Just's political philosophy as a "pastoral of politics (a vision of politics as a kind of neoclassical pastoral, with Rousseau as its Virgil)." And Finlay thinks of his garden, like David's paintings of Socrates and Marat, as being an act or deed, an assertion of moral and political principle.

If Neoclassicism provides the major part of Finlay's philosophical program, it is not the only source of his references. In his single-minded effort to keep alive as much as any one person can of the rich history of landscape painting and design, he draws on Claude Lorrain as much as Poussin; on Italian Renaissance and Roman villas; on Albrecht Dürer and Jean Baptiste Corot; on William Shenstone's garden, the Leasowes, and the Marquis de Girardin's garden at Ermenonville, which for a time was home to the beleaguered Rousseau and also for a time the place of his entombment. In so doing, Finlay has created not simply a landscape, but a tribute to art. He is reluctant, however, to have his garden identified as his only or even his principal activity. He wrote metrical poetry, short stories, and plays in the 1950s; in the 1960s he became involved with the concrete poetry movement which, with an extreme economy of language, substituted for metrical sequences of words the virtually solitary word as emblem and graphic image, replacing rhythm

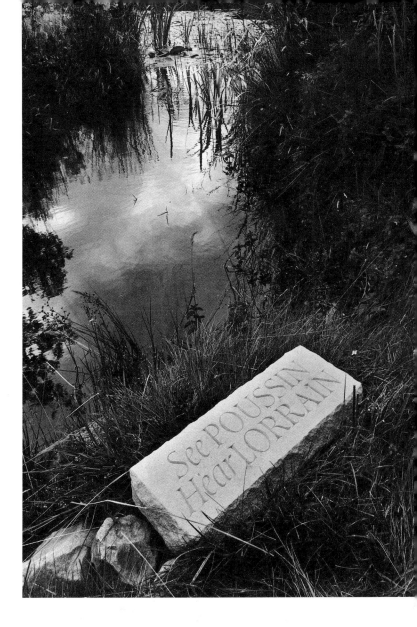

74. Ian Hamilton Finlay (with John Andrew).
See Poussin/Hear Lorrain. Stone. Stonypath.

with stasis. (This influence remains important in Finlay's garden work to this day.) Since his move to Stonypath in the winter of 1966–67, he has continued to publish books, prints, and pamphlets, as well as having his sculptural works realized elsewhere, chiefly at the Kröller-Müller Museum in the Netherlands and the Max Planck Institute in Stuttgart.

Finlay's work at Stonypath has been realized with the collaboration of his wife, Sue. When they began in 1967, Stonypath was little more than a collection of rough domestic and agricultural buildings surrounded by about four acres of moorland. Piece by piece and without a complete overall scheme, the Finlays began re-forming the site: transplanting trees and shrubs, damming and diverting streams to form ponds, moving earth and laying stones, and adding a variety of botanical specimens. This all transpired rather slowly, due as much to the Finlays' limited financial resources as to the pace of gardening activities. By now, the garden has matured considerably and contains several distinct sections: a front garden before the cottage; a courtyard garden with a small pond behind it in a space bordered by the old farm buildings (one of which has been converted into a garden temple); and a less intensively cultivated area beyond, with two more small ponds (upper and middle) and a larger one (Lochan Eck) leading into the moorland.[60]

Throughout this richly developed landscape, Finlay has arrayed his sculptural and poetic objects. Often made with the collaboration of various craftsmen, these have both a visual function, unifying the various parts of the garden, and a psychological one (like Pierce's works), arousing a variety of associations. The objects provide both visual and thematic unity. "Modern all-plant gardens are wholly lacking in harmony," Finlay asserts; "the entire Notion — in Hegel's word — is absent." Finlay's inscribed works are Neoplatonic emblems that can be "a) looked at, b) read,

c) ignored, d) read and meditated upon. Each, as one pleases, on the day." Thus something that can be used to provoke associations can also be appreciated solely for its visual character. Finlay underscores these multiple functions by saying, "All these works are works in themselves, as well as references, and (importantly) elements in larger compositions which include the plants."

Only a few of these works can be described here. In the front garden, a path formed of 71 diamond-shaped concrete slabs leads between borders of flowers and shrubs. On these slabs are engraved the names of different types of vessels — brig, keel, schooner, ketch — in one of Finlay's many references to the sea. Also in the front garden is a slate stele, *Wood Wind Song*, bearing three 72 different sequences of these three words. It stands in a grove of pines "which do indeed 'sing' with the wind which so often blows

75

here." Nearby, a large tree bears a plaque that reads *Mare Nostrum*, the Roman name for the Mediterranean and a tribute to this tree that is a source of sea sounds in Finlay's inland garden.

In one corner is an area that Finlay calls the *Roman Garden*: separated by cypresses from the rest of the front garden, it contains an 76 homage to the Villa d'Este in the stone form of a modern warship, which alludes to the use of carved galleys as decoration in Roman gardens and to their subsequent reappearance in the Renaissance, as at the Villa d'Este at Tivoli. In the courtyard garden this analogy 77 is continued with an aircraft-carrier fountain: a bronze warship spouts water, like the stone ships that are used to the same purpose on the terrace of the One Hundred Fountains at the Villa d'Este. In the courtyard 70 pond is a miniature landscape of marsh grasses and flowers, "signed" with a stone bearing Dürer's monogram and having the title *The Great Piece of Turf*. This is a living evocation of Dürer's watercolor of the same name (*Das Grosse Rasenstuck*), and a remark-

able composition in its own right.

This tribute — elegy, even — to Dürer has numerous parallels elsewhere in the garden. By the upper pond, overlooking a landscape of water and grasses and undulating hills, lies a stone bearing the inscription "See Poussin/ 74 Hear Lorrain." This is an invitation to meditate upon the landscape as it might have been depicted in the clearly ordered compositions of the former, or the more atmospheric, lyrical ones of the latter. Elsewhere, Finlay has placed a column base bearing the name of Rousseau at the bottom of a tree. The tree thereby becomes a living column, the whole a classicist tribute. A similar conceit lies behind the piece *Five Columns for the Kröller-* 75 *Müller*. There, a narrow path leads into a "secret garden" in a grove enclosed by rhododendrons, where five such column bases are placed against the trees. Each base is inscribed with a name: Corot, Lycurgus, Michelet, Robespierre, and Rousseau. The elegiac character of these works is reminiscent of elements in the now largely lost garden of the poet Shenstone. Along the

75. Ian Hamilton Finlay. *Five Columns for the Kröller-Müller*, 1982. Five trees with column bases in a grove. Garden of the Rijksmuseum Kröller-Müller, Otterlo, the Netherlands.

76. The Terrace of One Hundred Fountains at the Villa d'Este, a sixteenth-century garden at Tivoli, Italy.

77. Ian Hamilton Finlay. *Aircraft Carrier Fountain*. Bronze; approximate length: 3½ ft. Stonypath.

winding walk that circled his ornamented farm, Shenstone placed urns and seats dedicated to his friends, living and dead. He inscribed other seats with lines from Virgil and built a roothouse dedicated to a neighbor. There was a grove of trees also named for Virgil, and a grotto with a Latin inscription that evoked the Nereids. Even Shenstone's *Unconnected Thoughts on Gardening* (1764) finds an echo in Finlay's *Unconnected Sentences on Gardening* (see page 133), though Shenstone was different in stressing the supremacy of nature over art.

Fewer of Finlay's works are found by Lochan Eck, which lies the greatest distance from the house. On its shore, however, stands the unsettling *Nuclear Sail*. As Finlay explains this title, "Sailors call submarine conning towers 'sails,' and nuclear-powered subs 'Nuclear Sails.' " While Finlay's various aircraft-carrier sculptures utilize military imagery, this has a far more realistic scale and something of a malevolent character. In evoking terror and thereby triggering the instinct of self-preservation, this work adds an element of the sublime to the garden. It also provides an ironic comparison to the organic abstractions of Henry Moore, which are likewise often seen in the landscape.

"Certain gardens are described as retreats when they are really attacks,"[61] Finlay has written. Recently, his war on contemporary culture has taken a more literal turn. In 1978 the Strathclyde Regional Council withdrew discretionary rates relief on his garden temple. They claimed that only nonprofit art "galleries" are eligible for tax exemption; they insisted they had no category for art "temples" and his was thus subject to taxation. Finlay has refused to pay the rates, asserting that, like the garden, the temple has both artistic and spiritual purposes, despite the fact that its description confounds the Council. The temple is dedicated to Apollo and contains three chambers: one displays Finlay's

73

76

77

sculptural objects and publications; a second, a kind of indoor "sacred grove," permits a view out into the garden; and a third, inner chamber, lit only by candles, is a meditative space that suggests a cella.

To enforce their rates assessment, the Council sent a sheriff's officer to seize works of art for a warrant sale. On his first visit, the officer's car was barricaded in a "tank trap," and he retreated over the moors on foot. When he returned later in the day with the police to retrieve his vehicle, an imitation Panzer Mk IV erupted in a ball of fire and black smoke. He finally gained access to the garden temple, only to discover that the art works intended for seizure had been removed and hidden by Finlay's "Saint-Just Vigilantes." Video and still cameras recorded the action, while Scottish radio ran a live commentary on what Finlay now calls "The First Battle of Little Sparta (4 February 1983)."

Finlay's forces were less successful a month later when the sheriff's officer returned to take sculpture valued at 5,000 pounds, which was consigned to Christie's for sale. While Finlay and his supporters displayed considerable resourcefulness and not a little humor in these proceedings, one wonders how long he can hold out, physically and financially, in the face of bureaucratic hostility. The continued existence of environmental art works such as Finlay's is always a matter of great uncertainty. As a shrine to the intellect and the imagination, his garden seems particularly worthy of official sufferance, if not support.

It is a signal feature of recent art works in the landscape that their content is inclusive rather than exclusive, that they evoke history and memory as well as stimulating the eye. One might argue that Pierce and Finlay are no different from other land artists in this respect, and that their utilization of historically suggestive forms is no different from the archaisms of Holt or Morris or Heizer. But prehistory is only one small part of our past:

Pierce and Finlay are more far-reaching and even literate in their references. The use of history as an inspiration for contemporary art is more fashionable now than it was when Pierce and Finlay began their work in the late 1960s and early '70s. Yet prescience is the least compelling of their accomplishments. More than most other artists in the landscape, they demonstrate a complete grasp of the importance of appropriating and renewing the full richness of our cultural inheritance

If there are numerous historic and prehistoric sources for contemporary art in the landscape, there are also several distinguished twentieth-century antecedents. One of these is the remarkable sculptural environment created by Constantin Brancusi in the Romanian town of Tîrgu-Jiu, about 150 miles northwest of Bucharest. Brancusi (1876–1957) had lived in the town for a short time as a youth and was called back to create a memorial to local resistance to the Germans in the First World War. Brancusi accepted the commission in February of 1935 and made several visits to Tîrgu-Jiu from his home in Paris before his work was dedicated in 1938.

Brancusi's memorial consists of three major works and some lesser ones organized along an east-west axis running about three-quarters of a mile through the town. It begins in a park along the Jiu river with the *Table of* 79 *Silence*, a circular stone slab about seven feet in diameter and thirty-one inches high, surrounded by twelve stools, each of which has a round top and the shape of an hourglass. From there, a walk leads past square stools and benches, also designed by Brancusi, to the *Gate of the Kiss*. This is an architectural 78 elaboration of one of Brancusi's principal themes, which reaches back to 1908; it takes the form of a triumphal arch over seventeen feet high and twenty-one feet wide. It was carved in local travertine marble by an assistant under Brancusi's supervision. The lintel is inscribed with pairs of intertwined lovers, sixteen pairs on the front and back and four on each side, in a graphic shorthand variation on Brancusi's sculptural versions of the embrace. Each side of the supporting columns is divided vertically and carries near the top a large circular image that is an abstracted representation of the merged eyes of the lovers, but also an image of cell division as well as of male and female genitalia in sexual congress. Brancusi's triumphal arch thus suggests a dedication to the redemptive and procreative powers of love.[62]

From the *Gate of the Kiss*, a street was opened across town to the *Endless Column*. Named the Way of the Heroes, this street is bisected by the Church of the Holy Apostles and terminates at an open rectangle in which is centered the *Endless Column*. This is likewise a monumental adaptation of an earlier theme. It soars to over ninety-six feet in height and was made of iron cast from a wooden module, with the parts threaded over an internal steel post. Like an obelisk, it is at once an expression of aspiration and achievement; with its undulating surface, it draws the eye resolutely upward, like the spiraling frieze on Trajan's Column.

Research on Brancusi published in Romania confirms that he worked on the settings for all three of these sculptures.[63] He organized pathways and vistas, and arranged the seating. He specified the plantings of poplar and alder along the river near the *Table of Silence*. He dictated the length of the Way of the Heroes, seeing it as a metaphor for struggle: "The way of the heroes is always hard and long," he remarked.[64] A photograph of the site for the *Endless Column* reveals Brancusi's original thoughts for this work: on the photograph Brancusi has drawn his column surrounded by radiating pathways and groups of trees. "A monument depends on the precise place you choose for it, on the way the sun rises and sets upon it, on its surroundings," he wrote.[65]

Brancusi's project in Tîrgu-Jiu must surely be the most enigmatic of his works. In the West, it is undoubtedly the least known and discussed of the accomplishments of this widely celebrated artist. This is in some measure a reflection of Tîrgu-Jiu's remoteness from most observers. Yet it seems also an expression of the project's paradoxical relationship to the rest of Brancusi's œuvre: these are late works drawn from early themes; environmental works from an artist whose other sculptures appear so self-contained and unitary. Yet to Brancusi, the project represented a summing up. When he accepted the commission, he wrote, "Now all things begun long ago come to a close, and I feel like an apprentice on the eve of getting his working papers. So the proposal could not come at a better time."[66] Certainly the *Gate of the Kiss* and the *Endless Column* represent a kind of climax in Brancusi's work on these particular themes. But the quasi-functional and environmental character of the works at Tîrgu-Jiu are likewise the fulfillment of previous ideas.

Brancusi's studio had long contained architectural works: beams and archways, capitals and columns. As early as 1916 Brancusi executed a column bearing a version of the kiss motif. The Japanese-American sculptor Isamu Noguchi, who worked as Brancusi's studio assistant in 1927 while in Paris on a Guggenheim Fellowship, recalls seeing many of these works at the time and has testified to Brancusi's enthusiasm and talent for architectural sculpture. "What a pity," Noguchi remarked, "that he who had the greatest gift for architecture could not have found outlets other than the beautiful memorial in Romania."[67] Brancusi had likewise created sculpture based on functional forms. His wooden cups in particular seem a precedent for the utilitarian character of the *Table of Silence* and its surrounding stools. In addition, the careful creation of bases for his sculptures reveals that, to Brancusi, these objects were

80

intended to be seen as part of larger ensembles, in which all the parts were interdependent. Indeed, Brancusi created a whole environment of sculpture in his studio, which was preserved after his death and is now at the Musée National d'Art Moderne in Paris. From this environment of sculpture to the sculptural environment of Tîrgu-Jiu is perhaps not such a large step.

Given that Brancusi's work in Romania is not directly known to many contemporary artists, it is difficult to assess precisely its influence on recent landscape art. However, certain of Brancusi's sympathies were transmitted to the United States through Noguchi. He recalls Brancusi's emphasis on the perfection of form and surface, and on the appropriate use of tools. He also found in Brancusi's attitude toward nature something that was comparable to the Japanese: "Brancusi, like the Japanese, would take the quintessence of nature and distill it."[68] To Noguchi, Brancusi's work was never far from its cultural roots. When Brancusi came to Paris, Noguchi remarked, "He brought with him something more than learning: the memory of childhood, of things observed not taught, of closeness to the earth, of wet stones and grass, of stone buildings and wood churches, hand-hewn logs and tools, stone markers, walls, and gravestones. This is the inheritance he was able to call upon when the notion came to him that his art, sculpture, could not go forward to be born without first going back to beginnings."[69] These observations on Brancusi's sensitivity to his home environment, its landscape and vernacular traditions, are useful in any attempt to appreciate the success of his work at Tîrgu-Jiu; they serve equally as a reflection of Noguchi's own aesthetic philosophy.

Noguchi first saw Brancusi's work at an exhibition in New York in 1926, and he continued to visit periodically with the elder sculptor until Brancusi died in 1957. But while

Brancusi provides a distinguished precedent for Noguchi's ideas on sculpture and its environmental applications, he is not Noguchi's sole or even primary source. "I am a student of the use of sculpture in the past," Noguchi said recently. "Most of it is related to the use of architecture, from Michelangelo to the Greeks and the Egyptians. This was nothing special to Brancusi. It was just that he was aware of it, while perhaps some contemporary sculptors are not." Even before his time with Brancusi, Noguchi was demonstrating an independent view of sculpture, in which nature was paramount. He wrote in his Guggenheim application in 1926, "It is my desire to view nature through nature's eyes, and to ignore man as an object for special veneration. There must be unthought of heights of beauty to which sculpture may be raised by this reversal of attitude."[70] He sought, as he later told it, "a larger, more fundamentally sculptural purpose for sculpture, a more direct expression of Man's relation to the earth and to his environment."[71]

These convictions were strengthened by several experiences. Born in Los Angeles in 1904, Noguchi had lived in Japan from age two to fourteen. In 1930 he returned there for the first time since his youth. He discovered on that visit the inexpressibly beautiful temple gardens, with their compositions of rock and sand, moss and shrubbery, water and trees. These were to continue to have a profound influence on him. Noguchi made a more extensive world tour nearly twenty years later on a grant from the Bollingen Foundation, which he received in 1949 for the purpose of studying sculpture — primarily ancient — in its relation to its setting. In a two-year period, he visited Mayan ruins in the Yucatan; Stonehenge; Egypt; and the Observatories of the Maharajah Sawai Jai Singh II, the great sculptural toys built during the early eighteenth century in Jaipur.

Noguchi began making proposals for en-

78. Constantin Brancusi (1876–1957). *Gate of the Kiss*. Travertine; height: 17¼ ft., width: 21½ ft. Part of the monumental ensemble of sculpture at Tirgu-Jiu, Romania, executed between 1935 and 1938.

79. Constantin Brancusi. *Table of Silence*. Travertine; height: 31½ in., diameter: 7 ft. Tirgu-Jiu.

80. Constantin Brancusi. *Endless Column*. Cast iron; height: 96¼ ft. Tirgu-Jiu.

78

79

80

81

vironmental works as early as 1933. A model
81 from that year represents a *Play Mountain*,
conceived as a park and playground. The
same year he proposed a *Monument to the
Plough*, a vast earthen pyramid a mile on each
side, designed for a site in the Great Plains. It
was to be composed of furrowed earth and
planted with wheat on the sides and sur-
mounted with an enormous stainless steel
plow. "The model indicated my wish to be-
long to America, to its vast horizons of earth,"
Noguchi has explained.[72] It was his tribute to
the vast spaces and pioneer spirit of the West.
Though echoes of the past are evident in
these works, one cannot discount a certain
amount of social motivation. They were offered in the midst of the Depression, when
the social promise of modernist architecture
was likewise most pronounced. Noguchi
continued to press unsuccessfully for parks
and playgrounds, particularly for New York
City, well into the 1960s, continuing his efforts
at the artistic amelioration of the urban environment.

It was in the 1950s, outside of America, that
Noguchi finally saw some of his proposals
realized. He was commissioned to design two
bridges for Hiroshima in 1952 as part of the
reconstruction of that devastated city. Between 1956 and 1958 came his remarkable

garden for the UNESCO building in Paris, 82
which was designed by Marcel Breuer. Noguchi's garden is in two parts: an upper stone
terrace with square seats and carved boulders, and a lower area with mounded plantings, pools, paved and grassy areas. There are
distinctly Japanese elements in this garden:
natural stones set in raked gravel, for example, or stepping stones placed in the water. In
fact, some of the rocks were brought from
Japan. In consequence, Noguchi has called
this garden "my Roanji."[73]

This designation, however, better fits a
sunken garden executed on the Chase Man- 83
hattan Bank Plaza in New York City between
1961 and 1964. The landscape at Roanji, in
Kyoto, Japan, is best known for an enclosed
"dry stone" garden built in the late fifteenth
century. Fifteen stones in five unequal groups
are arranged asymmetrically in a bed of raked
gravel. No plants are included in this walled
garden except a little moss that grows around
the base of the rocks. This is a meditative
space, in which the simple stones are emblems of the larger world of nature and the
spirit, an idea that finds its Western equivalent in William Blake's *Auguries of Innocence*: "To see a world in a grain of sand/And
heaven in a wild flower/Hold infinity in the
palm of your hand/And eternity in an hour."

81. Isamu Noguchi (b. 1904). *Play Mountain*,
1933. Plaster and bronze; 4½ x 29¼ x 25¾ in.
Collection of the artist.

82. Isamu Noguchi. UNESCO gardens,
1956–58. Granite, grass, and foliage. UNESCO
Building, Paris.

83. Isamu Noguchi. *Chase Manhattan Bank Plaza Garden*, 1961–64. Black river stone, granite paving. New York.

84. Isamu Noguchi. *Marble Garden*, 1960–64. Marble. Beinecke Rare Book and Manuscript Library, Yale University, New Haven, Connecticut.

84

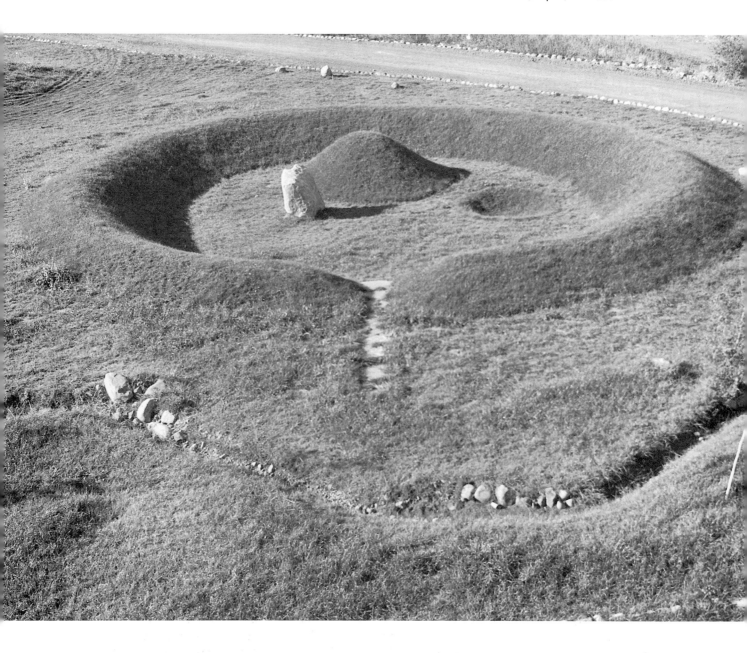

85. Herbert Bayer (b. 1900). *Earth Mound*, 1955. Earth; diameter: 40 ft. Aspen Institute for Humanistic Studies, Aspen, Colorado.

Noguchi's garden for the Chase Manhattan Plaza is likewise extremely economical in its forms. A few wildly eroded boulders scattered in a seemingly random pattern serve, as at Roanji, as the principal component of the composition. Concentric circles of granite paving stones replace the raked gravel of the earlier Japanese garden as the setting for the stones; these circles are interrupted by serpentine lines that add a suggestion of waves to the composition. This reference is strengthened in the summer months when the garden is flooded with a shallow layer of water, which spouts from two concentric rings of low jets. The boulders, brought from Japan, likewise carry a reference to water: their contorted shapes are the result of river erosion.

This garden was but one among many of Noguchi's projects that came to fruition in the middle years of the 1960s. Having waited so long to see more than the very occasional execution of his proposals for large-scale environmental works, Noguchi now began a period of enormous productivity. For the Beinecke Library at Yale University — a simple cube with a skin of translucent white marble designed by Gordon Bunshaft of Skidmore, Owings and Merrill — he created a beautifully consonant sunken plaza of white marble with a simple pyramid, a carved ring, and a cube perched on one point, all rising from the flat paving stones. For the IBM Corporation in Armonk, New York, Noguchi designed two gardens: one, representing the past, is a design of rough boulders among trees and grass; the other, representing the future, contains a pyramid of Brazilian granite, a black concrete dome inscribed with notations pertaining to nuclear physics and astronomy, an adjacent concavity of red concrete that serves as a fountain, and a bronze sculpture based loosely on the double helix form of the DNA molecule. And for the Israel Museum in Jerusalem, Noguchi designed a sculpture garden that includes both great undulating plazas contained by curved and sloping walls of stone rubble, and more intimate spaces for smaller sculptures framed by rectangular and circular concrete walls. Noguchi has continued this remarkable level of productivity to this day and has entered unreservedly into the discourse on the public purposes of art in the landscape, which will receive discussion in the following chapter.

Another artist of Noguchi's generation, Herbert Bayer, also executed environmental works that anticipate the recent effusion. The Austrian-born Bayer, who taught at the Bauhaus for several years in the late 1920s, emigrated from Berlin to New York in 1938, and moved to Aspen in 1946. There he worked as an architect and designer for the Aspen Development Corporation, participating in the planning for the Aspen Institute for Humanistic Studies. In 1955, on the grounds of Aspen Meadows, where guest housing for the Institute is located, Bayer created two environmental works. One is a *Marble Garden*, a composition of rough-hewn geometric elements freely placed around a square pool and fountain. The other, to contrast with it, is an *Earth Mound*. The *Marble Garden* takes the form of a predominantly vertical monument, while the *Earth Mound*, horizontal, forms a kind of enclosed precinct. The latter is forty feet in diameter and surrounds a low mound, a shallow conical depression, and a solitary standing stone. The references to Japanese gardens are apparent here, although particularly American forms such as corrals and Indian mounds have also been noted as sources.[74] That this work in turn provided some encouragement for younger artists is suggested by the fact that in 1968 its photograph was included along with the work of Heizer and Smithson in the Dwan Gallery *Earthworks* exhibition. Like Noguchi, Bayer was to continue to be of considerable significance in the development of the artistically improved public landscape.

84

85

86. Harvey Fite (1903–1976). *Opus 40*, 1939–76
(unfinished). Bluestone; 6.5 acres. Saugerties,
New York.

4. BEYOND LAND ART

Smithson was quick to recognize the limitations of the picturesque, at least in its more arcadian manifestations. He wrote in 1968: "The 'pastoral,' it seems, is outmoded. The gardens of history are being replaced by sites of time. Memory traces of tranquil gardens as 'ideal nature' — jejune Edens that suggest an idea of banal 'quality' — persist in popular magazines. . . . Could one say that art degenerates as it approaches gardening?" Continuing in a footnote, he asserted: "The abysmal problem of gardens somehow involves a fall from somewhere or something. The certainty of the absolute garden will never be regained."[75] Implicit here is Smithson's preference for landscapes that reveal the passage of time through successive episodes of human and natural upheavals, over those that conform to a preconceived notion of perfection. To Smithson, his preference was at once more appropriate and realistic. We have fallen from grace with the landscape, he implied. We have disrupted and degraded it. It is without the large unsullied vistas on which the picturesque depends. In such a time and such a landscape, Smithson asserted, the creation of artificial Edens is at best problematic, at worst a sham.

The picturesque encompasses far more than the pastoral; one of its many variants, most closely associated with the paintings of Salvator Rosa, shares in Smithson's infatuation with change, disorder, and decay. Yet in its most commonly understood form, the picturesque was no longer valid for Smithson. His aesthetic might instead be termed post-industrial: he accepted human disruption of the landscape and celebrated its renewal through reclamation works such as his own. Although one might quarrel with his complete repudiation of the picturesque — indeed, this survey provides ample evidence of its continued vitality — one must applaud his willingness to confront, even embrace, the problems of the contemporary landscape. In

his own way, Smithson provided a parallel to Noguchi's persistent efforts to bring additional parks and playgrounds to New York and other cities. The work of both artists affirms the socially beneficial aspects of landscape art, revealing an ever growing conviction that artists should be involved in the aesthetic decisions that are routinely made as a part of land use and urban planning, as well as land reclamation. This conviction has dominated much recent art in the landscape, inspiring numerous projects to reclaim industrial sites and renew urban spaces. Many of these efforts have been accomplished with partial government sponsorship, as was the case with Morris's *Grand Rapids Project*.

It would be misleading to say that the notion of art as land reclamation was solely the invention of Smithson and other avant-garde artists of his generation. Three decades before, a sculptor named Harvey Fite had unintentionally embarked on a project of a similar nature. In the late 1930s, Fite bought a deserted bluestone quarry in the Catskill Mountains of southern New York. It had been used as a source of building material and curbstones for New York City until it was abandoned at the turn of the century. Fite originally intended to utilize the quarry as a source of material for his representational carvings and as a place to exhibit them when complete. He began his work by building a stone ramp into the quarry, providing himself with access. Piles of unmarketable stone left behind by the nineteenth-century quarrymen were leveled, curving ramps and terraces were added until finally Fite's ambition for the quarry outgrew his original functional intentions.

Unlike Smithson or Morris, Fite worked virtually alone on his project, and used no heavy equipment — only the conventional stonemason's tools. As a consequence, his labor was prolonged. He cut each stone into a rectangular shape and placed stone upon stone

86, 87

87

with the short side forming the face of the walls. No mortar was used to secure them. Various natural features of the site were incorporated into the work: exposed bedrock was left uncovered, existing trees were kept in place, and groundwater that seeped through the rock was used to form pools at the lowest levels of the quarry. In the mid-1960s, a bluestone monolith was raised over the accretion of dry stone forms, giving a focal point to the serpentine forms. But even then, the work was not finished. Fite had worked some thirty-seven years on the 6.5 acre project by the time of his death in 1976 and had christened it *Opus 40*, anticipating that it would take four decades to complete.

Fite was without peers at the outset of his effort. His exemplars seem to have been the massive stone structures of the ancients, especially the Mayans, the Incas, and the Aztecs; he spent a year in Honduras restoring Mayan stone work in 1938, and in 1956 he went to Cambodia on a study grant from the Asia Foundation. But in the years since Smithson, Morris, and Fite first explored the utilization of art in land reclamation, the idea has attracted considerable support. The efforts of many individuals, artists and community leaders alike, coalesced in the summer of 1979 in a remarkable project in and around

Seattle, Washington, which went under the title *Earthworks: Land Reclamation as Sculpture*. Organized by the King County Arts Commission, the project was multifaceted. Seven artists were invited to propose art works for disused or abused sites in the Seattle-King County area.[76] The sites included a landfill, an eroded creek bed, three gravel pits, an abandoned naval air station, and a noise-control free zone surrounding the Seattle-Tacoma airport. The designs for all these proposals were exhibited for six weeks from August 17, 1979, at the Modern Art Pavilion of the Seattle Art Museum; during the same time, the Arts Commission hosted a symposium to discuss in detail the implications of the project.

As a practical demonstration, Robert Morris was selected to implement a proposal for a 3.7-acre abandoned gravel pit in southern King County. Morris presented a plan for the site in April of 1979, which was reviewed and subsequently approved by the King County Arts Commission and the County Department of Public Works. Construction was funded in part by the Art in Public Places program at the National Endowment for the Arts, the Department of Public Works, and the County Arts Commission; it began in August and was completed in November. The piece

86

88,89

87. Harvey Fite. *Opus 40*, aerial view. See plate 86.

88. Robert Morris (b. 1931). Untitled reclamation project, 1979. 3.7 acres. King County, Washington. A photograph taken shortly after construction.

89. Robert Morris. Untitled reclamation project, after seeding. See plate 88.

90, 91. Herbert Bayer (b. 1900). *Mill Creek Canyon Earthworks*, 1979–82. 2.5 acres. Kent, Washington. General view; dedication.

89

90

91

consists of concentric terraces and slopes forming an amphitheater in the center of the site, with a hill rising on the lower section. From within this amphitheater, only the sky is visible; from without, one looks over the largely rural Kent Valley to the distant Cascade Mountains. At the top of the slope, a few scattered tree stumps remain as emblems of resource utilization. In addition to demonstrating the artist's ideas on the aesthetics of art-as-reclamation, Morris's piece suggests the economic viability of this kind of art. County figures reveal that the Morris project cost little more than the lowest estimates for conventional reclamation of the site.[77]

Morris used the occasion of the symposium to express the hope, however, that reclamation works would not be promoted solely on the basis of their economics or their utility, but would be valued as art works as well. He also warned of the moral dilemmas that artists would face in undertaking these projects: that their work might be used to aid or disguise questionable resource development policies. "Will it be a little easier in the future," he wondered, "to rip up the landscape for one last shovelful of a non-renewable energy source if an artist can be found (cheap, mind you) to transform the devastation into an inspiring and modern work of art?" Recalling the commemorative function that was detected in Smithson's reclamation proposals, he observed that artists might not opt for disguise: "It would perhaps be a misguided assumption to suppose that artists hired to work in industrially blasted landscapes would necessarily and invariably choose to convert such sites into idyllic and reassuring places, thereby socially redeeming those who wasted the landscape in the first place." But he left the door open a crack. "There may be more choices available than either a cooperative or critical stance for those who participate."[78] Some degree of resource use is essential for life; the point is

that artists can help determine the wisest possible course. Standing apart from this effort and allowing sites to go unreclaimed is certainly no more moral than restoring a site developed under questionable motives or needs.

The King County Earthworks project had a significant spin-off in a scheme by Herbert Bayer that was realized in 1982 in the city of Kent, a Seattle suburb. Bayer, one of the seven artists selected for the project, designed a park containing a group of earthworks and a stormwater retention basin for a badly eroded canyon above the city. Development of land along the creek had resulted in an excessive flow of water during periods of heavy rain, and the city needed a way of containing it and allowing it to recede slowly through the town. Bayer's design provided them with a high berm that stops the water. Upstream is a group of earth forms that are inundated during times of flood and provide an inviting, 2.5-acre grassy park during dry periods.

The stream itself meanders through the site and has been lined with stone to discourage erosion. As it enters the park, it comes first to a mounded ring one hundred feet in diameter and five feet high, which it breaks with its passage. It then passes under a bridge that is poised between a berm and a conical mound. Another earthen ring is next, this one seemingly suspended in a circular pool of water eighty-five feet in diameter. This pond contains water part of the year, and drains at other times to reveal the full contours of the grass ring. Then comes the high berm, topped with another cone; below it is a final oval mound. Aware of the disruptive character of ordinary dams, Bayer sought instead to create one that would harmonize with its setting. "A dam in the ordinary sense constitutes a radical interference with the natural configuration of the land," he explained. "My intent was, therefore, to give the dams a

90–93

92

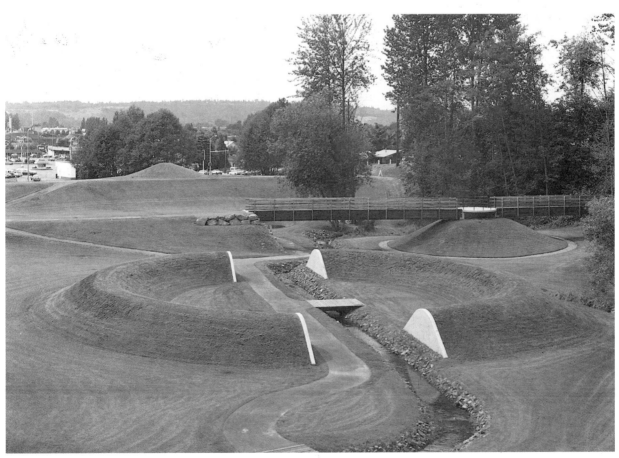

93

94. Michael Heizer (b. 1944). *Photomontage of Geometric Land Sculpture/Anaconda Project*, 1982. Projected dimensions: 400 x 5,000 x 400 ft., 1 million tons of rock. Anaconda Minerals Company.

natural appearance conforming to the landscape (surroundings) and to become integral parts of the landscape being created."[79]

Bayer's Mill Creek Canyon earthworks are the focal point of a one hundred-acre park that also includes a play area and a canyon trail. Their existence is a tribute to the enthusiasm and persistence of many in the Kent community. The total project cost came to $572,000, with $450,000 provided by the City Engineering Department to pay for the retention basin. The balance of $122,000 paid for the design and construction of the earthworks. This money came from a wide variety of sources, including the Kent Parks Department and Arts Commission, the King County Arts Commission, the Washington State Arts Commission, the National Endowment for the Arts, a Housing and Community Development Block Grant, and over 150 private donations of varying amounts from individuals and corporations. The city is understandably proud of the project, calling it "a landmark in park design, and a revolutionary concept in solving the problem of how to control surface water."[80] A concert by the Seattle Symphony was held in the park to celebrate the completion of the earthworks and the city has pledged to maintain them as part of the overall upkeep of the park area.

The small town of Hanna, Wyoming, displayed similar resourcefulness in commissioning sculptor Stan Dolega to participate in the reclamation of an abandoned surface coal mine. The site, some 120 acres in all, had been deserted since 1958; it was marred by piles of overburden, stagnant water, and an unauthorized dump. Hanna received a grant for reclamation from the Rural Abandoned Mines Program of the Soil Conservation Service, and a supplemental grant from the Art in Public Places program at the National Endowment for the Arts to incorporate earthworks designed by Dolega. He concentrated his sculptural forms, completed in 1981,

on a twenty-acre parcel of the abandoned mine owned by the state. Working with the existing spoils piles, he recontoured them into a sequence of geometric terraces that link two areas of different elevations. He describes these forms as being "inspired by the flattened buttes typical of the high plains."[81] "The Soil Conservation Service will try to revegetate the sculpture," Dolega added, "but the soil has been severely damaged." An authorized landfill was established on the site: Dolega planned its contours so that they would merge with those of his earthwork after its expected twenty-five-year period of use. Recreational facilities, including a shooting range and a dirt-bike course, were also incorporated into the reclamation scheme.

Several other projects are tangentially related to reclamation efforts. In Nevada, Michael Heizer is working with a mining company that is moving staggering quantities of earth to extract molybdenum. Heizer has convinced them to allow him to use thirty percent of the overburden to construct long, horizontal benches, including several pyramidal forms. 94 The execution of this work depends on the continued economic health of the mining operation; it may never see completion. Heizer insists, in his typically recalcitrant way, that the principal aim of this effort is not reclamation. "It's getting my art out into the real world, where I've always wanted it to be." And of his continued preoccupation with the Western landscape, he will say only: "It's where I live."

In upstate New York, sculptor William Bennett is utilizing a partially exhausted limestone quarry as a site for a massive environ- 95–97 mental work. His purpose is not expressly reclamation; instead, he talks of the quarry as a "found object" and a "powerful space." He has been fascinated by quarries since his days as a graduate student at Indiana University in the early 1970s, when he took his art into the limestone pits around Bloomington. There he

95. William Bennett (b. 1948). *Jamesville Quarry Sculpture*, work in progress. *Wedge (Stone Boat)*, begun 1976. Limestone; 80 x 10 x 6 ft. *Inverted Pyramid* (proposed). 160 x 160 x 20 ft. Jamesville, New York. Photomontage by the artist.

96. William Bennett. View looking into *Wedge (Stone Boat)*.

97. William Bennett. View from within *Wedge (Stone Boat)*.

95

98

96

97

98. Joseph Kinnebrew (b. 1942). *Grand River Sculpture*, 1975. Concrete; 45 x 35 x 30 ft. Grand Rapids, Michigan.

99. Patricia Johanson (b. 1940). *Fair Park Lagoon: Pteris Multifida (Planting Plan)*, 1982. Ink, pastel, and conté crayon on paper; 36 x 30 in. Rosa Esman Gallery, New York.

began work on a carved relief that soon grew off the single wall onto many others and onto the floor of the pit. In the New York quarry, Bennett has dug his work into the ground. Thus far, it consists of a long, triangular wedge that begins at ground level, drops to a depth of six feet and widens to ten. Opposite the point of this wedge, Bennett plans to excavate an inverted pyramid 160 feet square and 20 feet deep, from the bottom of which will rise another, smaller pyramid, this one pointing back to the sky. Recalling the prolonged efforts of Harvey Fite, Bennett has painstakingly lined the floor and walls of the wedge with cut limestone slabs; he plans the same surface for the pyramidal forms. And like Fite, he works in his quarry on his own and only in the warm months. During the rest of the year, his sculptural production includes stone works that frequently take an architectural form.

Finally, Michigan sculptor Joseph Kinnebrew has created an architectural sculpture that is an example of reclamation only in the broadest sense of the word. His work is more properly described as an effort at environmental restoration or renewal. A dam in the Grand River at Grand Rapids had been preventing spawning fish from moving farther upstream. The Michigan Department of Natural Resources had plans to build a simple, entirely functional fish ladder when Kinnebrew approached them with a proposal to elaborate and improve the structure. Kinnebrew's fish ladder, completed in 1975, added walkways, seating, and viewing platforms, providing spectators with overlooks of the river, the dam, and the spectacle of migrating fish. And within days of its completion, spawning trout were found over one hundred miles upstream. This project was sponsored by the Arts Council of Greater Grand Rapids, with funds from the Department of Natural Resources, the National Endowment for the Arts, the Michigan Council for the

Arts, and several local private foundations.

Clearly, the use of art in land reclamation and environmental restoration is an idea that has fired many imaginations. Other projects are in the planning stages. For a lagoon in Dallas's Fair Park, New York artist Patricia Johanson has proposed creating two intriguing painted concrete forms based on types of local aquatic vegetation, which will help stabilize the eroding shoreline while adding colorful paths and bridges over the water. In Minnesota, sculptor Andrew Leicester has proposed to the Iron Range Resources and Rehabilitation Board that they work together in creating a commemoration to mining activities in the now economically depressed Mesabi Range. Michael Heizer has been approached by Ottawa Silica Company about reclaiming a one hundred-acre surface coal mine in Illinois. One senses that an enthusiasm for this sort of work comes less from some quixotic yearning of the artist to feel needed than from a pressing awareness — among artists and the general public alike — of the complex problems generated by continued exploitation of natural resources. The potential of art to assist in the renewal of landscape has been demonstrated; it needs now to be developed to the greatest possible advantage.

While these artists have been elaborating the utilization of art in land reclamation, others have been evolving strategies for different kinds of public works. Generated by the same sense of commitment to improving public spaces, these include the creation of parks, playgrounds, and plazas. In large measure, their public purposes have been matched by public support, through the National Endowment for the Arts, the General Services Administration, state and local arts councils, and numerous other public organizations. This public support is in numerous cases matched by private financial and in-kind contributions. Many of these public

98

99

organizations have already been noted as supporters of reclamation efforts, but they have also played a significant role in developing other possibilities for environmental art in the public space.

It is Noguchi who provides the most dramatic example of the multiple purposes of this art. Noguchi has been the recipient of numerous commissions, both public and private; they have been awarded both for environmental designs and for discrete sculptural objects. Among the former are the projects for Chase Manhattan Bank and Yale University mentioned in the last chapter. Among the latter are his tubular steel *Sky Gate* in Honolulu, the majestic *Portal* at the Justice Center in Cleveland, and the massive granite *Black Sun* in Volunteer Park, Seattle. While Noguchi's environmental commissions in the 1960s were often private, those in the 1970s were frequently public.

In 1975, for example, the same year that *Sky Gate* was erected in Honolulu, the High Museum in Atlanta approached Noguchi with the idea of creating a play environment in Piedmont Park. The city provided a site within the park that was in need of restoration and secured an Art in Public Places grant; the museum assumed the responsibility for matching the grant, which they accomplished with the assistance of local foundations and charitable organizations. At the time of the Atlanta commission, only one of Noguchi's playground proposals, which date back to the 1930s, had been realized, and that was in Japan. His project in Atlanta places the play sculptures inside a low wall, which protects the playground from the street and also screens out some of the traffic noise. Under a ring of mature oak trees, Noguchi arrayed a group of brightly colored, sturdy play shapes — including slides, swings, cubes, mounds, and several structures for climbing — which are intriguing to children and adults alike.

For the Art in Architecture Program of the General Services Administration (GSA), Noguchi created that same year one of his gardenlike spaces. In front of a new Federal Building in Seattle is his *Landscape of Time*, 103 lightly carved stones set into a brick plaza and interspersed with trees. The time alluded to in this landscape is of several measures, as is often the case with environmental art works. There is first of all the great scale of geological time implicit in the ancient stones; there is also the measure of human history suggested in Noguchi's imaginative reuse of a venerable Japanese garden tradition.

It is in Detroit that Noguchi's talents in environmental design have received their fullest expression, at least to date. In 1970 Noguchi was asked to submit a proposal for a fountain as part of the plans for a new Civic Center Plaza, bounded by the Detroit River on one side and commercial development on the other, and within sight of Renaissance Center, symbol of the city's commitment to urban revitalization. Noguchi developed a fountain design and submitted it together with some suggestions for adjusting the plaza plans to better accommodate his fountain. His suggestions fell on receptive ears, and he was taken on to reform the entire eight-acre site.

Hart Plaza, as it is known, is disposed over 100 two levels. It includes restaurant and performance facilities beneath, and open paved and green areas above, together with a large amphitheater that doubles in the winter as a skating rink. At the center is Noguchi's extraordinary fountain, a sculptural and tech- 101–2 nological marvel. It is composed of a tubular ring held twenty-four feet off the ground on two legs, which rise out of a shallow round basin. The flow of water is completely computerized: several dozen programs create a seemingly infinite variety of water patterns generated from above and below, from a fine mist to a massive aquatic column. At the entrance to the plaza is another sculptural object, a twisting aluminum pylon that rises to a height of 120 feet. Both this gleaming column and the computerized fountain have a deliberately machine-tooled, futuristic look. "I wanted to make a new fountain, which represents our time and our relationship to outer space," Noguchi observed.[82] The technological metaphor is also appropriate to a city that is home to the industry that has transformed American life in the twentieth century: the automobile. But the fountain is technology transformed: "a machine becomes a poem," as Noguchi himself put it.[83] It is proof of Noguchi's continued sculptural inventiveness, while the larger plaza is witness to his sensitivity to the need for physical relief from the claustrophobia of the inner city, which is the most welcome aspect of the new public space. "What is important above all," Noguchi stresses, "is the sense of space that Hart Plaza supplies. An opening to the sky and to the Detroit River. A horizon for people."[84]

Detroit asked for a fountain and received an entire plaza; Miami wanted a new bandshell and may be on the way to a completely new look for Bayfront Park, which lies between the bay and Biscayne Boulevard, one of the city's principal thoroughfares. Despite its central location, the park is underutilized and run-down. Noguchi saw the park and be-

came convinced that the renewal of the antiquated bandshell would not be adequate to correct the park's problems. He sought and received approval to prepare instead a master plan for eighteen of the park's acres. His proposal calls for the removal of an old library building and the addition of an amphitheater, fountains, a children's playground, and a bayside walk, all contained within low berms that would protect the park from the noise and congestion of Biscayne Boulevard. Noguchi's plans contain design elements for which he has a demonstrated ability; the City Commission voted final approval of them in October 1980 and hopes to implement them over a period of years.

Few artists have received the number of commissions or the broad mandate accorded to Noguchi. But others have been engaged in similar kinds of projects. In Rosslyn, Virginia, for example, Nancy Holt was retained to create a small park at one of the major points of entry into this commercial district just across the Potomac River from Washington, D.C. Her plans, implemented in late 1983, included a high berm pierced by a tunnel entrance and embracing a number of sculptural elements: concrete spheres perched in or near small pools of water, serpentine walls and paths. The berm itself spills into the entry

104

101, 102. Isamu Noguchi. Views of Horace E. Dodge and Son Memorial Fountain, 1978. Stainless steel with granite base; height: 24 ft. Hart Plaza, Detroit.

103. Isamu Noguchi. *Landscape of Time*, 1975. Granite; 5 elements, height of tallest rock: 8 ft. Federal Building, Seattle, Washington.

101

102
103

plaza of the adjacent building, the design of which was modified at Holt's request. Sight lines in the berm and several of the concrete globes focus attention on the relationships among the spheres. Originally, county planners had thought to have the park and sculpture designed separately. But the artist selection panel, reacting to the extremely small site (about one-half acre), felt that park and art work needed careful integration, and recommended Holt as an artist capable of executing a single unified design for both sculpture and open space.

In Dallas, meanwhile, Robert Irwin successfully added in 1980 a sculptural element to a gateway park designed by the landscape architecture firm of Sasaki/Walker. He was presented with a puzzling site, carved up by several roads, and the all but completed plans for the park. He responded by suggesting a twelve-foot high steel wall that would slice through the hilly site, unifying the various divided parcels. In places, Irwin's wall is entirely visible; at others, it nearly disappears into the mounds. It is broken at street cross-

ings and pierced to allow pedestrian passage.

And in Seattle, five artists have worked together on the grounds of the new National Oceanic and Atmospheric Administration building. The five — Siah Armajani, Scott Burton, Doug Hollis, Martin Puryear, and George Trakas — have each created sculptures that are connected along a path. Hollis has fabricated a sound garden: organ pipes that resonate in the wind. Burton's work is a terrace and viewpoint overlooking Lake Washington, while Armajani's consists of two stone bridges inscribed with quotations from Moby Dick, appropriate to this waterfront site and the mandate of NOAA. Armajani, a sculptor of considerable accomplishment and great potential, has also submitted to the Maryland State Arts Council an intriguing proposal for a poetry garden. With minimum disruption to an existing site, stones inscribed with poetry would be disposed around the landscape, creating a meditative garden that might well recall the work of Ian Hamilton Finlay.

The involvement of artists in the design of public space has required some modification

105

104. Nancy Holt (b. 1938). Park project for
Rosslyn, Virginia, work in progress. ½ acre.

in their working methods. For many of these projects are public not only in the final sense of being of free and easy access, but in the planning process as well. Public presentation by the artists of their previous work, hearings on their proposals, review by engineers and landscape architects: these procedures are familiar to architects, perhaps, but until recently, less so to sculptors. Artists have also been drawn into collaborative situations with each other and with other professionals, most particularly architects and landscape architects. These collaborations are uneasy at best: there may well be something irreconcilable in the crisp, thorough methods of architects, for example, and the more intuitive, empirical methods of artists. At the Massachusetts Institute of Technology, however, a successful instance may be developing in the design of a new visual arts building by I. M. Pei. Several artists are cooperating with him on specific aspects of the project, including Richard Fleischner, who is involved in the creation of an outdoor space adjacent to the building. Fleischner has simultaneously designed a courtyard of trees, teak benches, and marble blocks for the new Dallas Museum of Fine Arts.

It remains to be seen, however, if any real rapprochement can occur between artists and other design professionals. There is some reason to wonder if this is even entirely desirable: if art is thoroughly subsumed under other disciplines or a completely functional intent, it is bound to lose some of its particular magic. What is needed is some balance between art and utility, as demonstrated by Noguchi in Detroit or Holt in Rosslyn. Yet the impulse to collaborate arose out of a genuine sense that contemporary art, when introduced to the public environment, too often looked out of place, embarrassed, even naked. Twentieth-century art has been almost without exception a private art; museums have been the protective escorts of

its public debut. To suddenly take the most recent expression of this privately generated art and insert it into the public space is bound to cause discomfort all around, for most recent art is entirely without the commemorative functions or narrative content of traditional public art. It is no wonder that artists and art organizations have sought a healing of the breach between private art and public context through collaborations with those more accustomed to operating in the public arena.

But collaborations represent only one way of closing the gap. Indeed, a great deal of the recent history of the environmental art movement can be read as an effort to restore to art some of its centrality in public discourse, to "get art out into the real world," as Michael Heizer would have it. Often, this effort has been pursued with just that same private vocabulary that the public has long found so baffling. But with the utilization of art in land reclamation or park design has come the merging of art with identifiable functions in an effort to render the art not just physically approachable, but emotionally and intellectually accessible as well. This is a matter of great delicacy: again, there is the threat of the art's becoming merely utilitarian. But in the absence of any commemorative function, narrative content, or commonplace iconography, one recognizes that some measure of usefulness certainly eases the difficult passage of contemporary art into the larger world. One wonders at times if the environment — particularly in the cities — really needs additional visual clutter in the form of sculptural objects, no matter how well intentioned. With so apparent a need for urban restoration and land reclamation, the purposeful aims of much recent environmental art may represent the best possible future for public art in this country.

One final aspect of recent art in the landscape remains to be examined. This one is

105. Robert Irwin (b. 1928). Untitled project for East Portal Park, 1980–81. Cor-ten steel; length: 700 ft. Dallas, Texas.

106. Richard Fleischner (b. 1944). Project for the new Dallas Museum of Fine Arts, work in progress. Limestone, marble, wood, and plantings; 115 x 115 ft. Dallas, Texas.

107. Richard Serra (b. 1939). *Spin Out (For Robert Smithson)*, 1973. Hot rolled steel; 3 plates, each 10 ft. x 40 ft. x 1½ in. Rijksmuseum Kröller-Müller, Otterlo, the Netherlands.

106

107

perhaps the most puzzling of all, in the sense that it is the most difficult to define. It is the phenomenon generally known as sited sculpture. As the term implies, these are three-dimensional objects carefully situated in their surroundings. This is not in itself a new idea: traditional sculpture applied to architecture or monuments centered in public squares certainly can be said to be sited. Yet much modern sculpture, as suggested above, has had a rootless character. It has been a thing unto itself, concerned with its own internally generated form and the properties of its own materials. It has been sustained by the neutral, characterless space of the museum and gallery. Land art helped restore to sculpture a sense that the surroundings — and most particularly the landscape — were all-important both in the formulation of a work and in its perception. Sited sculpture emerged in the wake of this restoration, and can be said to have descended in part from land art. More often than not, sited sculpture is placed in the public domain. It therefore partakes in the debate about the public purposes of recent art in the landscape. Without such evident utilitarian aims, however, the public benefit of sited sculpture is often more heatedly debated.

Land art, to review, is in large measure about the landscape itself — its scale, its vistas, its essentially horizontal character, its topography, and its human and natural history. It is frequently made from the materials at hand. It reveals the changing characteristics that a work assumes in different conditions: diurnal or nocturnal light, winter glare or summer haze, full sun or cloud shadow. While any outdoor work will change appearance under different conditions, sited sculptures are less exclusively about the landscape itself. They are also about mass, form, volume, surface: that is, some of the traditional concerns of sculpture. Alternatively, they are manifestations of the organization of space,

both internal and external: that is, architecture. They are still made with a great sensitivity to the surroundings — and often, this is the landscape — but have an internal coherence that land art does not. With sited sculptures, there is often an explicit boundary between the work and the environment. Rather than being forms that have emerged from the landscape, they have the look of objects that have been set down within it.

Looking back over some of the projects discussed in the initial chapter of this book, one can see the distinctions between land art and sited sculpture emerging even in the early 1970s. Nancy Holt's *Sun Tunnels*, for example, are industrial forms introduced into the landscape, displaying far more of an interest in surface and in positive form than the earlier *Double Negative*, which was composed of empty space. One can also see the phenomenon of sited sculpture emerging in the work of artists not generally associated with land art. Richard Serra is one of these. His sculpture is often formed of massive, rusted steel plates that intrude upon and alter the space in which they are placed, proclaiming their materiality through demonstrations of mass, balance, and stress. Occasionally, these sculptures have been made very successfully outdoors. In a wooded glen at the Kröller-Müller Museum in the Netherlands, for example, Serra dedicated a work from 1973 to the memory of Robert Smithson. Entitled *Spin Out (For Robert Smithson)*, it consists of three standing plates in a centrifugal arrangement, which disappear into the surrounding slopes. The length and shape of each plate is determined by the contours of the natural setting. Conversely, the plates describe a horizontal cross section of the landscape, like orthogonals in a perspectival rendering. This reciprocity brings *Spin Out* as close as Serra ever came to the aims of the land artists.

Carl Andre is another who sometimes took

107

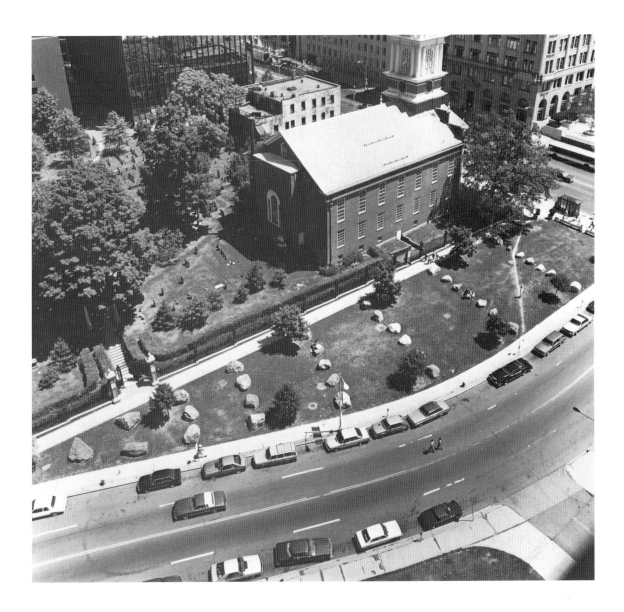

his sculpture outdoors. In a controversial 1976 commission for Hartford, Connecticut, he arranged thirty-six glacial boulders in eight rows on a triangular site. At the apex stands a single stone, the largest of the group. The second row is composed of two slightly smaller boulders; the third, three that are smaller still. This pattern of increased number/decreased mass is continued through the eight rows. As the numbers increase, so does the interval between the rows. Andre's work often depends on just such mathematically determined groupings, but his materials are more often industrial, metallic, and modular. Out of a respect for this outdoor setting, he shifted to an irregular, natural material; from a sense of the awkward site emerged the triangular form of the work. This *Stone Field Sculpture* also makes reference to a nearby

cemetery: Andre wanted to create a work that would "extend the serenity of the graveyard."[85] Like *Spin Out*, it is an example of the subtle differences between the environmentally determined sculpture and the sculptural manipulation of the environment itself.

Andre's *Stone Field Sculpture* was not welcomed gently to its appointed site. Blasted in letters to the editor in the local press, it quickly became an issue in the 1977 mayoral campaign. It was criticized for its price ($100,000) and its use of coarse, unworked elements. The controversy eventually spread to the *New Yorker*, the *St. Louis Post-Dispatch*, and *Time* magazine. A similar storm blew up in Seattle over Michael Heizer's sculpture *Adjacent, Against, Upon*. Completed in 1976, it is sited in Myrtle Edwards

109. Michael Heizer. *Adjacent, Against, Upon,* 1976. Concrete and granite; overall: 9 x 130 x 25 ft. Seattle, Washington.

110. Beverly Pepper (b. 1924). *Amphisculpture,* 1974–77. Concrete; 8 x 270 x 14 ft. Bedminster, New Jersey.

111. Athena Tacha (b. 1936). *Streams*, 1976. Pumice, rocks, sandstone, and lake pebbles; 10 x 20 x 30 ft. Vine Street Park, Oberlin, Ohio.

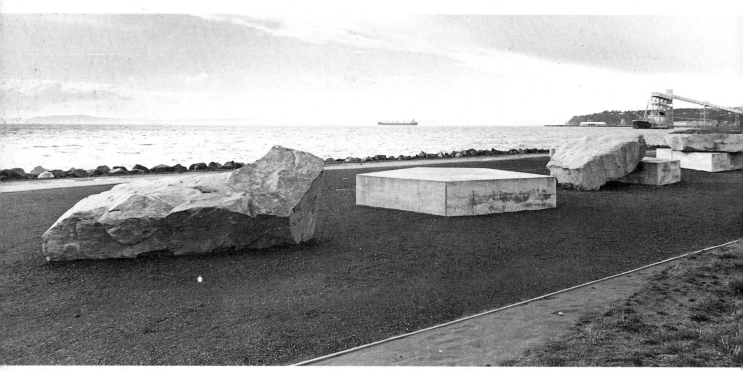

109

Park on the Seattle waterfront. It is a combination of natural and architectonic elements — massive granite slabs quarried in the Cascade Mountains, resting near, leaning against, and set upon concrete plinths that are variously three-, four-, and five-sided. As such, the work mediates between the natural and architectural landscapes that compose the view from the site: Puget Sound and the distant Olympic Peninsula in one direction, the city in the other.

Controversy notwithstanding, sited sculptures have become the frequent objects of both corporate and public commissions. Heizer has recently completed a fountain, *Levitated Mass*, for the IBM Corporation in New York. A granite slab seems to hover over a bed of rushing water; the fountain's location — Fifty-sixth Street at Madison Avenue — is indicated in carved, cryptic inscriptions on the stone and continued on the stainless steel frame. For its office building in Bedminster, New Jersey, A.T.&T. commissioned a sculpture from Beverly Pepper in 1974. Titled *Amphisculpture*, Pepper's work consists of 110 concentric terraces stepping down into a shallow bowl that is bisected by sloping walls and platforms of concrete. The whole, some 200 feet in diameter, evokes the form of a classical theater. Athena Tacha's *Streams*, 111 commissioned by the city of Oberlin, Ohio, in 1976, likewise draws on a classical vocabulary, in this instance, stone terraces or steps. Tumbling down a slope on the banks of a creek in a city park, it throws off classical regularity through the syncopated placement of risers and treads. Some risers are higher than others; some steps longer or wider. Scattered throughout are irregular boulders that elaborate the visual rhythms of the steps. Both

Pepper's and Tacha's works, in the manner of much sited sculpture, combine built form with the use of landscape contours.

Nancy Holt and Richard Fleischner are two others who have subsequently distinguished themselves in the creation of sited sculpture. The particular appeal of Holt's work lies in its knowing attempt to reconcile formally distinct, quite architectural sculptures with their surroundings. This is most often achieved through the use of sight lines that lead the eye out into the landscape.

113, 114   Holt's *Rock Rings* was commissioned by Western Washington University and stands on a wooded edge of the campus in Bellingham. Constructed of schist quarried in nearby British Columbia, it is composed of two concentric walls of stone that are perforated with archways and portholes. These windows provide framed vistas over the adjacent meadows and into the trees; the arches are oriented in a north-south direction. The work thus has the effect of placing the observer in the environment. At the same time, however, the strongly architectural character of the work separates inside from outside, creating a cloistered space. One has the sense of being in a secret garden, from which it is possible to look out without being seen. The same effect was produced in a piece commissioned on the occasion of the Thirteenth Olympic Winter Games. Standing in an open

115, 116   field near Lake Placid, Holt's *Thirty Below* is a slender cylinder of brick, thirty feet high and just over nine feet in diameter. Two arches on

a north-south axis allow entry to the piece at ground level. To the east and west sides, low berms lead up to slotted windows that look into and through the piece. From within it, one's principal vista is up, from the darkened interior out to the sky. Shafts of light are thrown upon the inner walls by the perforations of *Thirty Below*: as with the star holes of *Sun Tunnels*, forms in light are caught and projected.

Holt has since done a number of pieces in a thin black steel that resembles wrought iron. These retain an architectural character, while being far less massive than the stone, concrete, or brick pieces. *Inside/Outside: N.W., Washington, D.C.* took the insistent dome of federal ceremonial architecture and opened it up to the air, both through the lattice structure and the circular openings in the steel. And *Wild Spot*, on the campus of Wellesley College in Massachusetts, made literal the notion of environmental protection. The piece is composed of two rings of steel fencing. The outer one is broken to allow access to the piece, but the inner one is continuous, enclosing a patch of indigenous wildflowers.

Fleischner has also explored the creation of outdoor spaces, but in a way that is at once more subtle and less architectural. In Roger Williams Park in Providence, Rhode Island, Fleischner built a small bridge over a canal to Cow Island, where he created an environment out of discreet stone elements. Several of these are arrayed along a dominant axis, which conforms to an existing path on the is-

112. Nancy Holt. *Annual Ring*, 1980–81. Steel
bars; height: 14 ft. 3 in., diameter: 30 ft.
Federal building, Saginaw, Michigan.

land. Climbing the gentle slope, one comes first to a pink granite slab that is the threshold to the piece; continuing on, one encounters at the crest of the island an open square paved with the same pink granite. From there, two parallel bars of black granite lead down the other side of the island, hugging the ground. To either side of the main square are several other subsidiary elements: a short black granite column to one side balanced by a pink one on the other, and a pair of pink granite steps. Through the combination of all these components, Fleischner brings a remarkable degree of spatial organization to the two-acre island in an elegantly unobtrusive manner.

For a new Social Security Administration building in Woodlawn, Maryland, Fleischner created a similar environment of sculptural forms in 1980. Commissioned by the General Services Administration, the piece occupies a three-acre site. But while Cow Island is relatively open, the Woodlawn site is thickly wooded. Fleischner responded by increasing both the vertical dimensions and the mass of his components. They are again arranged around a central element: in this instance, a platform of rusted steel held horizontal above a slight grade. Up the slope is a kind of portal 117 formed of two facing right angles of pale granite, with a threshold before them. Down the grade, one confronts a high wall of standing steel plates. Hidden behind it is an enigmatic 118 granite cube, like a windowless blockhouse. To one side, serving to lure visitors into this environment, are two sets of four tall columns, one on the edge of a grassy area adjacent to the Social Security building, the other slightly into the woods. On the other side is a small plinth and an inverted arch. Again, Fleischner has achieved a deft orchestration of these different elements — vertical and horizontal, granite and steel—and an intriguing balance between passage and closure. He demonstrates an ability more common to

landscape architects than sculptors to activate space through just the right proportional and compositional relationships among elements widely scattered in a landscape.

The aspect of sited sculpture easiest to separate from land art is that which is most specifically architectural. Siah Armajani has created a number of wooden structures he describes as "reading gardens," with indoor spaces for reading or meditation, but without much obvious relationship to the landscape. Mary Miss and Alice Aycock have both experimented with constructed forms as well. But even architectural structures can bear a significant relationship to their physical and cultural settings. An intriguing case in point is a project by Andrew Leicester for Frostburg State College in Maryland. Frostburg lies in Allegany County, in the mountainous western panhandle of the state. As the site of the first bituminous coal-mining operations in the United States, the region is richly endowed with remains of the industry's 120-year history. Commissioned by the Maryland State Arts Council to create a sculpture for the college campus, Leicester elected to erect a memorial to miners.

Prospect V-III, as Leicester's work is known, 119–22 was completed in 1982. It is a wooden structure over 120 feet long and 27 feet high, combining multiple elements that recall the architecture of mines and mining towns. At the outer extreme is a viewing platform that rises above a steep slope and overlooks the George's Creek basin, historical center of the region's coal operations. At the inner extreme is a narrow mine shaft dug for the piece, which serendipitously terminates in a coal seam discovered in the digging. In between are several chambers resembling miners' cottages and detailing the life of the miner. In the first is a coal cart that is also a cradle, set on tracks 121 that lead irrevocably into the mine. It is surrounded by painted butterflies that metamorphose into black lungs, a reference to the

113, 114. Nancy Holt. *Stone Enclosure: Rock Rings*, 1977–78. Stone masonry; height: 10 ft., diameters: 40 ft., 20 ft. Western Washington University, Bellingham, Washington.

115, 116. Nancy Holt. *30 Below*, 1980. Brick; height: 30 ft., diameter: 9 ft. 4 in. Mr. and Mrs. Henry Uihlein, Lake Placid, New York.

117, 118. Richard Fleischner. *Baltimore Project*, 1980. Granite and cor-ten steel; 3 acres. Social Security Administration Center, Woodlawn, Maryland.

113

114

115

116

117

118

119

crippling miner's disease. A second represents the miner's maturity, and evokes the tomblike chambers that the miners dig in the coal seam. A third displays the memorabilia of mining, including picks, shovels, and lunch pails as well as photographs and documents. Much of this material, which was intended to suggest the retirement of a miner, was donated to the project by miners, their widows, and families in a gesture of support and enthusiasm for the memorial.

120 Between this third chamber and the mine shaft is a hexagonal "rotunda," built to resemble a changing room, with working clothes suspended in the skylit dome. Partially buried in the hillside, it also suggests an archaic beehive tomb. Mining terms are stenciled on the walls, together with glyphs from the Egyptian Book of the Dead. Entrance to the simulated mine is from this final chamber; the shaft is held up by wooden posts and lintels. The cart tracks disappear into the blackness. Glancing back, one overlooks the

119 whole length of the piece and out into the valley.

In addition to receiving donations of mining equipment and memorabilia, Leicester was assisted in planning this memorial by local miners. Septuagenarian Tony Urbas was

one of these. "This is something the area has been in need of, something in memory of the miners who worked the area," Urbas told a newspaper reporter. Frostburg College President Dr. Nelson P. Guild agreed with him. "This is about the first thing that has ever been done in this area in recognition of the life of the coal miner," Guild said.[86] There is a special poignance to the placement of this memorial on the campus of Frostburg College. A history of the school reveals that in the late nineteenth century, miners in the Frostburg area were stopped as they left the pits and asked to make contributions for a Normal School. Their donations went toward the purchase of the land on which the college now stands. Adjacent to it is a modern strip mine, the mechanized replacement of the deep pits in which these miners labored. Leicester's *Prospect V-III* demonstrates with particular intelligence the fact that commemorative content, like a purposeful intent, can ease the introduction of contemporary art into the public domain and enhance the public purposes of art in the landscape.

Because much recent environmental art has come into being with at least partial public sponsorship, one might forget that on occasion it is still realized through entirely

119. Andrew Leicester (b. 1948). *Prospect V-III*, 1982. Wood and mixed media; height: 27 ft., length: 123 ft. Frostburg State College, Frostburg, Maryland.

120. Andrew Leicester. The Rotunda, leading into the mine shaft at *Prospect V-III*.

121. Andrew Leicester. The first cottage at *Prospect V-III*.

private means. Christo, in his typically exaggerated way, reminds us of this: though his works are public spectacles, they continue to be financed through the private sale of his drawings, collages, and sculptures. Moreover, they continue to engender controversies that are large in proportion to their permanence and in excess of their real threat to the environment. It may be that this is simply a function of the flamboyance of his projects and their immodest budgets; no doubt it also follows from the vast quantities of publicity that this artist's enterprises invariably generate. When he proposed recently to install 11,000 banners on twenty-five miles of pathways in New York's Central Park, even the *Public Interest* and the *New York Times* threw themselves into the fray.[87] A *Times* editorial on March 5, 1981, commended the Parks Department for denying Christo a permit to execute this piece, on the grounds that it ran counter to the department's policy of decreasing abuse and encouraging restoration of the park. They also noted that the project's anticipated cost of five million dollars was more than the annual maintenance budget for the park and more than five years' worth of restoration funds. One has to question this moralizing over the cost of a project that was to be privately funded and that might have lent a festival air to a small corner of that grim city. Would it not have been more productive to issue Christo the permit on the condition that he make a substantial contribution to the park's restoration funds?

When Miami granted Christo a permit to surround with 200 feet of floating pink polypropylene eleven of the city's fourteen islands in Biscayne Bay, they received an environmental bonus. Christo agreed to donate $100,000 to Dade County for the Biscayne Bay Preservation Fund, and $50,000 to the City of Miami. In addition, before the vivid pink fabric was unfurled for two weeks in May of 1983, the armies of Christo's workers cleared the is-

123, 124

120

121

122. Andrew Leicester. Entrance into the Rotunda at *Prospect V-III*.

123, 124. Christo (b. 1935). *Surrounded Islands*, 1983. Woven polypropylene; 6½ million square ft. Biscayne Bay, Greater Miami, Florida.

123

124

lands of every scrap of trash. There was an element of self-interest in this: Christo wanted his pink to contrast with the unbroken blue-green waters of the bay and the uncluttered greenery of the islands. He also announced an intention to surround only those islands in the bay that were man-made (the result of dredging a shipping channel), leaving the natural ones unmolested. And he made the usual arrangements for a study of his project's potential threat to the environment, under pressure from a small but vocal group who feared that it would endanger manatees and nesting birds. A section of the pink fabric was floated over an aquarium tank containing manatees; not only did it not disturb them, but it apparently inspired them to amorous activities.[88]

Like Christo's other projects, *Surrounded Islands* was a grand gesture, but civil and even humble in its impermanence. Six and a half million square feet of the woven fabric was folded and attached to pink styrofoam booms, which were towed out to the islands. The booms were anchored 200 feet offshore, and the fabric pulled to land, across the beach, and hooked to earth anchors driven in under the cover of vegetation. The fabric was specially sewn to follow exactly the contours of the islands, except in two instances where Christo surrounded two islands in a single group. The fabric came alive in the water, billowing in the waves and the small tide. One participant recalled seeing a dozen pelicans fly in low over his island and turn a hot pink from the reflection. "That moment was like magic," he said. "And it just might pass for art."[89]

Two more recent works will serve as a coda for this survey. One is entirely private and temporary, the other a public monument intended for the ages. One is best described as a three-dimensional painting in the landscape, the other as a work of landscape architecture that is also a contemporary sculpture.

Both are thus hybrids, demonstrating the fusion of forms that has come in the wake of artistic experimentation in the past decade and a half. But beyond that, they reveal just how significant and pervasive have the forms and attitudes of land artists become in recent years. What began in the late 1960s as a rejection by just a handful of artists of the then current forms of art has developed into a phenomenon that touches many of the most consequential aspects of art today, from land reclamation to the improvement of public spaces. That recently the impact of land art can be felt in the practice of painting and landscape architecture as well only confirms that it has sounded a major chord in contemporary culture.

Alan Wood is a British-born Canadian painter living in Vancouver. Over the past several years, his work has become increasingly three-dimensional. At first, this development amounted only to the application of collage or relief to canvas, but eventually Wood began to build environments out of his paintings, constructing forms of canvas-covered wood that were painted and installed in museum and gallery spaces. At the same time, his subject matter moved from the abstract to the increasingly naturalistic. In particular, he began to draw on the features of his adopted British Columbia landscape: its cathedrals of trees, its waterfalls and mountains, its ocean fronts.

In 1980 Wood made his first visit to the Cariboo, the vast, semiarid interior of British Columbia. Having been nurtured on Hollywood westerns as a child in the industrial town of Widnes, near Liverpool, Wood immediately recognized in this landscape the features that had fired his imagination as a youth and that he knew still formed the dominant myth of the West, both in the United States and in Canada. There were the wide open spaces, the sagebrush, and the distant mountains. There, too, were the deserted frontier towns and farmhouses, the irrigation troughs and the snaking fences, the windmills and water tanks. To Wood, the vernacular ranch architecture he encountered was to western Canada "as the Parthenon is to Greece or Elizabethan or Georgian architecture is to Britain": something indigenous and altogether remarkable. The result of this inspiration was an installation at the Emily Carr College of Art in Vancouver in 1981. It included a gate, a corral, a chute, piles of fencing, and an actual fence row disappearing into an illusionistic landscape. All were fabricated of canvas wrapped around wooden supports and colorfully painted.

Wood's enthusiasm for the Western myth did not end there. In 1982 he determined to 125–28 create an elaborate tribute to ranch architecture, this time in the landscape itself. With the support of many individuals in Vancouver and across Canada, funding was secured and a site was found. Throughout the winter and early spring of 1983 Wood and his crew were busy in a warehouse on the edge of Vancouver, fabricating the components of his three-dimensional painting. These included a life-size water tank and windmill, barns of different sizes, gates, and miles of fencing. Constructed of over 150,000 board-feet of lumber, the components were then knocked down and fed through a homemade machine that wrapped them in a continuous strip of canvas and bathed them with a coat of primer paint. Loaded on flatbeds, these stacks of brilliantly colorful elements were trucked over the Rocky Mountains to Alberta in the late spring.

There, they were reassembled at a working ranch about twenty miles west of Calgary. Approaching the 320-acre site, one was greeted by the sight of a large horse and rider crashing down a hill out of the trees. Like all the components of Wood's *Ranch*, this was made of painted canvas pulled over a wooden frame. From there, one arrived at a large corral and two small pens at the en-

trance to a large triangular valley. Painted fences ran east and west. To the west lay three kinds of haystacks, again made of canvas-covered wood. One was in the shape of rolled hay, one suggested bales, and the third alluded to the vertical cones that were painted by Claude Monet.

To the east were several other tableaux. On a rolling hill, a seven-bar fence was painted to resemble a rainbow. Below was a blue and yellow bridge and a group of stark white geometric shapes that Wood described as a "still-life": a pyramidal windmill, a cylindrical 126 water tank, and a conical and cylindrical feeding trough. Nearby stood five "receding" barns. They ranged from full size to miniature 127 and were arranged from large to small to simulate diminution over a large distance. The color scheme intentionally confounded this appearance, however: the largest was a cold bluish-white, while the others ranged through a pale blue and mauve to pink and bright red.

From the barns, a trail led east past three tepees to a group of "old West" façades, in- 128 cluding store fronts, hitching posts, and a boardwalk. The façades were held up at the back by an obvious framework, in an explicit reference to movie sets. Two other groups of Western buildings were nearby: a small church with a graveyard and picket fence, and a pioneer homestead, complete with cabin, fence, gate, and outhouse. In the distance, three huge canvas birds seemed to hover over a hilltop, while a fan-shaped installation was meant to suggest the circular fields formed by irrigation from a single, central source. Finally, hidden in the trees was a piece Wood called *Ranchenge*: this was a 125 purple, blue, and orange corrallike structure composed of two concentric circles of posts and beams, some standing and others falling. It was inspired both by Stonehenge and by the decaying ruins of an actual corral that Wood had seen on a visit to the Cariboo.

125. Alan Wood (b. 1935). *Ranchenge*, from *Ranch*, 1983. Wood and painted canvas. Near Calgary, Alberta.

126. Alan Wood. A tableau entitled *Geometry*, including a windmill, a water tank, and feed troughs, from *Ranch*.

127. Alan Wood. *Five Receding Barns*, from *Ranch*.

128. Alan Wood. Storefront façades and church in township, from *Ranch*.

127

126

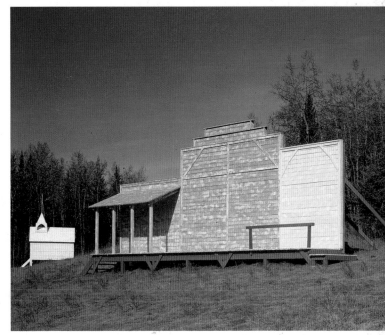

128

129. Maya Lin (b. 1959). *Vietnam Veterans Memorial*, 1982. Black granite; height: 10 ft., length of each wall: 250 ft. Constitution Gardens, Washington, D.C. View of the apex of the two walls.

129–32 No more different a tribute from Wood's could be imagined than the Vietnam Veterans Memorial. Completed in the autumn of 1982, the memorial provoked a national drama that reproduced in microcosm the conflict engendered by the war itself. Conceived by veterans and paid for with private donations to the Vietnam Veterans Memorial Fund, it is nevertheless an entirely public monument: authorized by Congress, placed on public land, and commemorating the more than 57,000 individuals who died at the request of their government.

The memorial is an elegantly simple one. Its form is an open V-shape with an interior angle of 132 degrees. It is set into the ground, with walls of polished black granite holding up the earth behind it and facing a gradual grassy slope that climbs back up to Constitution Gardens, the Mall, and the other national memorials. The sloping ground gives the walls an elongated, triangular form, as if they were emerging from or receding into the earth in the manner of the Serra in Holland or the Irwin in Texas. On the face of the walls are the names of all those who died or are still missing-in-action in the Vietnam War. The names are given chronologically, beginning at the top right of the Memorial's apex, continuing to the far right and then jumping to the extreme left, and culminating at the bottom left of the apex. In the words of Maya Ying Lin, who designed this memorial as a Yale undergraduate student: "Thus the war's beginning and end meet; the war is 'complete.'. . . yet broken by the earth that bounds the angle's open side, and contained by the earth itself."[90]

Lin's design was unanimously selected by a jury from over 1,400 entries submitted in an open competition for the memorial. Competition rules specified, among other things, that the names of the dead and missing should be included in the memorial, and that it should be "contemplative and reflective in character." Lin's design fulfills these requirements with brilliance. Set into the earth, it is sheltered from the ceaseless noise of nearby Constitution Avenue, creating a space that is profoundly calm despite the frenetic surroundings. It is an environmental rather than a conventionally monumental work: its principal axis is horizontal rather than vertical. It accords with its setting in a subtle yet knowing way: the two walls form sight lines that lead directly to the Washington Monument in one direction and the Lincoln Memorial in the other. These are both visual and symbolic links. They give the memorial an emphatic sense of belonging on the site, and a contextual continuity with the earlier monuments. To be sure, this is a different sort of memorial: horizontal while those are vertical, black while those are white, spatial while those are architectural. But this commanding alignment allies the Vietnam Memorial with those earlier commemorations of valorous service to the nation.

The best memorials have always had a cathartic function, easing trauma into memory. In this, especially, the Vietnam Veterans Memorial is a stunning success. It is the continual witness of tearful homages to the deceased. Flowers and mementos are regularly left there. These visible expressions of grief are eloquent demonstrations that the individual and collective wounds of Vietnam are still raw, and in need of remedy. The controversy that surrounded the commission was itself a part of a much-needed catharsis. A group of the veterans felt that the memorial was demeaning: they interpreted its blackness and its in-ground setting as implicit condemnations of the war and the sacrifices it required. They were also puzzled by its reductive character — its simple geometry, its abstractness, its unobtrusive horizontality — all of which seemed too much like modern sculpture. Yet Maya Lin's design is in a distinguished tradition of funerary tablets, and no

130. Maya Lin. *Vietnam Veterans Memorial*.
View looking down wall.

131. Maya Lin. *Vietnam Veterans Memorial*.
Closeup view of stele with mementos left at
the memorial.

130

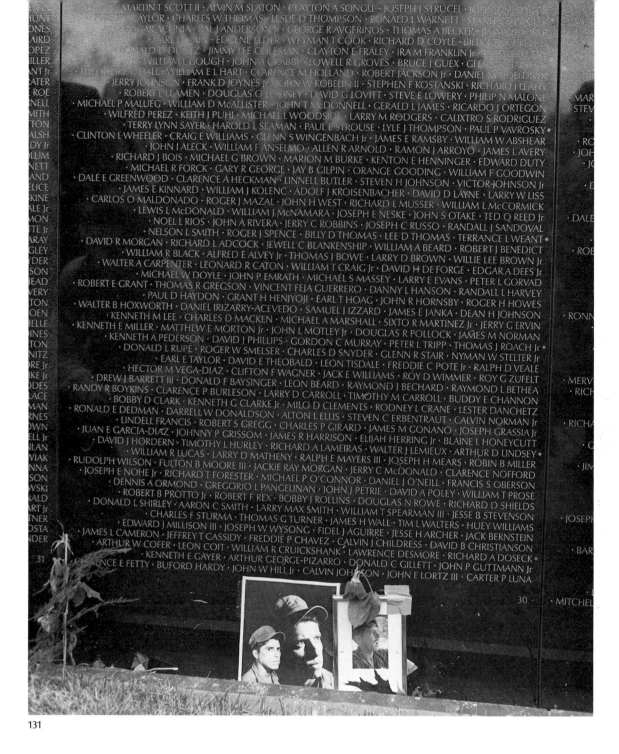

131

more "abstract" than the Washington Monument. Its blackness and inscribed names serve simply to remind us that people die in wars, irrespective of their cause. As the architecture critic of the *Washington Post* wrote, "Black is indeed the color of sorrow and of mourning, but not of shame."[91] Lin's memorial commemorates sacrifice and death; its perceived antiwar imagery has less to do with her design than with the continued national conflict about the moral rightness of the war. If we were united in our approval of the war, there would be no cause to look for antiwar sentiment in what is, in any case, a morally neutral statement.

As a concession to those who disapprove of the memorial, plans were approved to place a figurative sculpture at its entry. A grove of trees just away from the end of one of the black walls was chosen as a site for an eight-foot-high bronze sculpture of three infantrymen. Ironically, this may prove to be the more abstract element of the ensemble, divorcing the commemoration from the sacrifice of known individuals. These idealized figures cannot provoke the same sense of wrenching, sorrowful recognition provided by Maya Lin's funerary stele. One imagines that ultimately, once the wounds of Vietnam have healed, the memorial will transcend its specifically commemorative function and stand as an eloquent tribute to all those who have died in our nation's wars, for whom there is no other memorial in the capital.

Scarcely more than a dozen years separate *Double Negative* from the Vietnam Veterans Memorial. If they seem to bear little resemblance to each other, consider this: that they are both meditative spaces, the one a problematic gesture toward the majesty of the earth, the other a recognition of its hal-lowed function as the receiver of our dead. In between has come an unbounded exploration of the use of art in the landscape to both utilitarian and transcendent ends. If only the Vietnam Veterans Memorial were to endure from this period of brilliance, that would be accomplishment enough. But we have seen more and can rightfully hope for its continuation: the restoration of our urban spaces and the reclamation of our postindustrial landscapes, and the renewal through less specifically utilitarian works of our appropriate sense of awe and respect for the extraordinary character of the land.

NOTES

1. John Beardsley, *Probing the Earth: Contemporary Land Projects*.

2. Ralph Waldo Emerson, "Nature," 1836, in Brooks Atkinson, ed., *The Complete Essays and Other Writings of Ralph Waldo Emerson* (New York: Modern Library, 1950), p. 34.

3. Thomas Jefferson, "Notes on Virginia," 1782, in Paul Leicester Ford, ed., *The Writings of Thomas Jefferson* (New York: G. P. Putnam's Sons, 1894), vol. 3, p. 271.

4. Ibid., p. 268.

5. Those who have read J. B. Jackson's excellent essay, "Jefferson, Thoreau & After," will recognize my indebtedness to him here. *Landscape* 15 (Winter 1965–66): 25–27; reprinted in Ervin H. Zube, ed., *Landscapes: Selected Writings of J. B. Jackson* (Amherst: University of Massachusetts Press, 1970), pp. 1–9.

6. Henry David Thoreau, "Walking," in Henry S. Canby, ed., *The Works of Thoreau* (Boston: Houghton Mifflin, 1937), pp. 659–60.

7. For a thorough treatment of the breadth of Olmsted's achievement, see Albert Fein, *Frederick Law Olmsted and the American Environmental Tradition* (New York: George Braziller, 1972).

8. Unless otherwise noted, all quotations are from conversations with the artists.

9. Michael Heizer, "The Art of Michael Heizer," p. 34.

132. Maya Lin. *Vietnam Veterans Memorial*. View toward the Washington Monument, photographed at the dedication ceremonies, November 11, 1982.

10. Quoted in Howard Junker, "The New Sculpture: Getting Down to the Nitty Gritty" p. 42.

11. Heizer, "Art," p. 37.

12. Published in Robert Hobbs, *Robert Smithson: Sculpture*, p. 238.

13. Joseph Masheck, "The Panama Canal and Some Other Works of Work," p. 41.

14. Michael Auping, "Michael Heizer: The Ecology and Economics of 'Earth Art,'" *Artweek* 8 (June 18, 1977): 1.

15. Quoted in Douglas Davis, "The Earth Mover," *Newsweek*, p. 113.

16. Discussed in Elizabeth Baker, "Artworks on the Land," p. 94.

17. Others in this exhibition included Richard Long, Robert Morris, and Dennis Oppenheim.

18. From Alexander Pope, "Epistle to Lord Burlington," 1731.

19. Particularly curious are his characterizations of the picturesque theories of Uvedale Price as a "democratic dialectic between the sylvan and the industrial," and of Olmsted's work as a "Jeffersonian rural reality in the metropolis." See Robert Smithson, "Frederick Law Olmsted and the Dialectical Landscape," *Artforum* 11 (February 1973): 62–68; reprinted in Nancy Holt, ed., *The Writings of Robert Smithson*, pp. 117–28.

20. Originally published in Gyorgy Kepes, ed., *Arts of the Environment*, pp. 222–32; reprinted in Holt, *Writings*, pp. 109–16. All quotations from the latter source.

21. Robert Smithson, "A Sedimentation of the Mind: Earth Projects," *Artforum* 7 (September 1968): 45; reprinted in Holt, *Writings*, p. 82.

22. Samuel Beckett, quoted by Smithson in his film *Spiral Jetty*, and used by Liza Bear and Nancy Holt in "Robert Smithson's Amarillo Ramp," pp. 18–19.

23. Smithson, "Spiral Jetty," in Holt, *Writings*, p. 111.

24. See Robert Smithson and Gregoire Müller, ". . . The Earth, Subject to Cataclysms, Is a Cruel Master," *Arts Magazine* 46 (November 1971): 36–41; reprinted in Holt, *Writings*, pp. 179–85.

25. Smithson, "Untitled, 1971," in Holt, *Writings*, p. 220.

26. Smithson, "Proposal, 1972," in Holt, *Writings*, p. 221.

27. Smithson, in Holt, *Writings*, p. 220.

28. Robert Morris, "The Art of Existence, Three Extra-Visual Artists: Works in Progress," *Artforum* 9 (January 1971): 28.

29. Robert Morris, "Aligned with Nazca," p. 39.

30. Robert Morris, "Some Notes on the Phenomenology of Making: The Search for the Motivated," *Artforum* 8 (April 1970): 66.

31. In *Grand Rapids Project: Robert Morris*, n.p.

32. Ibid.

33. Quoted in *The Golden Door: Artist-Immigrants of America, 1876–1976*, exhibition catalog (Washington, D.C.: Hirshhorn Museum and Sculpture Garden, 1976), p. 389.

34. See Alfred Frankenstein, "Christo's 'Fence,' Beauty or Betrayal?" pp. 58–61.

35. Nancy Holt, "Sun Tunnels," p. 36.

36. I should say that a comparable sensibility was not unknown to America during the same years. Dennis Oppenheim, for example, drew a line in the snow on the frozen St. John River on the border of the United States and Canada, which disappeared as the ice melted. He directed the seeding of a field of grain in Holland in 1969 and then disrupted its harvest in a piece that lasted as long as the growing season. But a more aggressive aesthetic soon took hold in America, making Oppenheim something of an outsider; he went on to create elaborate indoor constructions. Ironically, his more modest approach was to seem prescient a half-dozen years later, as other American artists — Michelle Stuart and Michael Singer among them—opted for more subtle works. But it was in England that this sensibility flourished.

37. Unless otherwise noted, quotations from Richard Long are from a statement published in *Aspects of British Art Today*, exhibition catalog (Tokyo: Asahi Shimbun, 1982), p. 174.

38. Richard Long, *Five, Six, Pick Up Sticks, Seven, Eight, Lay Them Straight* (London: Anthony d'Offay, 1980), n.p.

39. Quoted in Michael Auping, "An Interview with Hamish Fulton," in *Common Ground: Five Artists in the Florida Landscape*, p. 87.

40. Unless otherwise noted, quotations from Hamish Fulton are from a statement published in *Aspects of British Art Today*, p. 115.

41. Quoted in Auping, "Interview," pp. 86–87.

42. Unless otherwise noted, quotations from David Nash are from *Loosely Held Grain*, exhibition catalog (Bristol: Arnolfini Gallery, 1976), n.p.

43. See Shenstone's interview with James Thompson, included in John Dixon Hunt and Peter Willis, eds., *The Genius of the Place: The English Landscape Garden 1620–1820* (London: Elek, 1975).

44. From a statement in *Fletched Over Ash*, n.p., published on the occasion of Nash's exhibition at AIR Gallery, London, 1978.

45. Quoted in Hugh Adams, "Natural Acts," in *Sixty Seasons: David Nash*, p. 27.

46. Originally published in Charles Simonds, *Three Peoples* (Genoa: Samanedizione, 1975); reprinted in John H. Neff, *Charles Simonds*, pp. 35–38.

47. Rémy Inglis Hall, trans., *The Wandering Jew and Other Stories* (London: Hart-Davis, 1967), pp. 3–14.

48. See Robert Goldwater, *Primitivism in Modern Art* (New York and London: Harper and Brothers, 1938; revised New York: Vintage Books, 1966).

49. Arshile Gorky, from a letter dated February 17, 1947; reprinted in K. Mooradian, ed., "A Special Issue on Arshile Gorky," *Ararat* (New York) 12 (Fall 1971): 39.

50. Barnett Newman, from the announcement of an exhibition at Betty Parsons Gallery, New York, in 1947; quoted in Ralph Pomeroy, *Stamos* (New York: Harry N. Abrams, 1974), p. 19.

51. Adolph Gottlieb and Mark Rothko, from a letter to the editor, *New York Times*, June 13, 1943, sec. 2, p. 9.

52. See especially the essays and selections of artists' writings in *The Natural Paradise: Painting in America 1800–1950*, exhibition catalog (New York: Museum of Modern Art, 1976).

53. Christopher Hussey, *The Picturesque* (New York and London: Putnam's, 1927; reprinted Hamden, Conn: Archon Books, 1967), pp. 58–59.

54. For thorough discussions of the sources of the picturesque, see Hunt and Willis, eds.,

The Genius of the Place, and Christopher Hussey, *English Gardens and Landscapes 1700–1750* (London: Country Life, 1967).

55. Recent speculation on the iconographic program at Stourhead is summarized in Kimerly Rorschach, *The Early Georgian Landscape Garden*, exhibition catalog (New Haven: Yale Center for British Art, 1983), pp. 75–77.

56. Ian Hamilton Finlay, "Unconnected Sentences on Gardening," in *Nature Over Again After Poussin*, p. 21.

57. Unless otherwise noted, quotations from Finlay are from correspondence with the author.

58. The exhibition was held at Collins Exhibition Hall, University of Strathclyde, Glasgow, in 1980.

59. Stephen Bann, "Introduction," in *Nature Over Again After Poussin*, p. 9.

60. A more complete description of Stonypath can be found in Stephen Bann, "A Description of Stonypath."

61. Finlay, "Unconnected Sentences on Gardening," p. 22.

62. For a more extended discussion of this theme, see Sidney Geist, *Brancusi: The Kiss*.

63. See Barbu Brezianu, *Brancusi in Romania*, pp. 128–154.

64. Quoted in Brezianu, p. 130.

65. Quoted in Brezianu, p. 131.

66. Constantin Brancusi, from a letter dated February 11, 1935, quoted in Geist, *The Kiss*, p. 76.

67. Isamu Noguchi, "Noguchi on Brancusi," p. 29.

68. Quoted in Sam Hunter, *Isamu Noguchi*, p. 35.

69. Noguchi, "Noguchi on Brancusi," p. 29.

70. Isamu Noguchi, *A Sculptor's World*, p. 16.

71. Noguchi, *A Sculptor's World*, p. 159.

72. Quoted in Hunter, *Noguchi*, p. 56.

73. Quoted in Hunter, *Noguchi*, p. 111.

74. Jan van der Marck, *Herbert Bayer: From Type to Landscape*, p. 40.

75. Smithson, "A Sedimentation of the Mind: Earth Projects"; reprinted in Holt, *Writings*, pp. 85–86, 91.

76. The artists were Herbert Bayer, Iain Baxter, Richard Fleischner, Lawrence Hanson, Mary Miss, Dennis Oppenheim, and Beverly Pepper.

77. Total project costs (excluding indirect costs) on the Morris project were $145,800; estimates for conventional reclamation ranged from $132,000 to $190,000. Figures from a report by the King County Arts Commission to the National Endowment for the Arts; reported in Dolores Tarzan, "Earthworks Are Good Economics," *Seattle Times* (October 17, 1979), p. A8.

78. Robert Morris, "Robert Morris Keynote Address," in *Earthworks: Land Reclamation as Sculpture*, p. 16.

79. Quoted in "Dedication of Earthworks Park in Kent Is September 4," *The Arts* 11 (newsletter of the King County Arts Commission, August 1982): 2.

80. From a press release of the Kent Parks and Recreation Department, August 13, 1982.

81. From an undated press release prepared by Stan Dolega.

82. Quoted in Nancy Foote, "Sightings on Siting," in *Urban Encounters: Art, Architecture, Audience*, p. 32.

83. Quoted in Hunter, *Noguchi*, p. 165.

84. Quoted in *Isamu Noguchi: The Sculpture of Spaces*, p. 29.

85. Quoted in Diane Henry, "Some Residents of Hartford Are Throwing Stones," *New York Times*, September 5, 1977, p. 21.

86. Both quotes are from an Associated Press story, "Former Coal Miner's Dream Comes True with Monument Dedication at Frostburg," circulated from Baltimore, October 11, 1982.

87. See Nathan Glazer, "Christo in Central Park—And in Harlem," *Public Interest*, no. 68 (Summer 1982), pp. 70–77, and "Closing Christo's Gates," *New York Times*, March 5, 1981, p. A22.

88. Reported by William Dunlap, a painter from McLean, Virginia, who worked on the project.

89. William Dunlap, "Surrounding of Island 12," *Washington Post*, May 15, 1983, p. K5.

90. Quoted in Benjamin Forgey, "Model of Simplicity," p. C4.

91. Benjamin Forgey, "Monumental 'Absurdity,'" *Washington Post*, March 6, 1982, p. C5.

ARTISTS' STATEMENTS

Walter De Maria

The Lightning Field

Some Facts, Notes, Data, Information, Statistics and Statements:

The Lightning Field is a permanent work.

The land is not the setting for the work but a part of the work.

The sum of the facts does not constitute the work or determine its esthetics.

Because the sky-ground relationship is central to the work, viewing *The Lightning Field* from the air is of no value.

Part of the essential content of the work is the ratio of people to the space: a small number of people to a large amount of space.

It is intended that the work be viewed alone, or in the company of a very small number of people, over at least a 24-hour period.

The light is as important as the lightning.

The period of primary lightning activity is from late May through September.

There are approximately 60 days per year when thunder and lightning activity can be witnessed from *The Lightning Field*.

The invisible is real.

The observed ratio of lightning storms which pass over the sculpture has been approximately 3 per 30 days during the lightning season.

No photograph, group of photographs or other recorded images can completely represent *The Lightning Field*.

Isolation is the essence of Land Art.

Walter De Maria, "The Lightning Field," p. 58.

Ian Hamilton Finlay

Unconnected Sentences on Gardening

A garden is not an object but a process.

Flowers in a garden are an acceptable eccentricity.

Poussin and Salvator: Cops and Robbers.

Modern sculpture is *wilfully* ignorant.

Ethical Battles are 18th Century Gardens continued by other means.

What our culture proposed as the *general* it now treats as an eccentricity.

Ecology is Nature-Philosophy *secularised*.

Technology—Epic Convenience.

The murmur of innumerable bills was known to most great gardeners.

Superior gardens are composed of Glooms and Solitudes and not of plants and trees.

Weather is the chief content of a garden.

Installing is the hard toil of garden making, *placing* is its pleasure.

Garden centres must become the Jacobin Clubs of the new Revolution.

Public funding of the arts should be confined to nations with heroic ideologies.

Grand conceptions are inhuman to small inhuman minds.

Certain gardens are described as retreats when they are really attacks.

Our earth is carnivorous.

Embark on a garden with a Vision but *never* with a plan.

Ian Hamilton Finlay, *Nature Over Again After Poussin*, pp. 21–22.

Richard Fleischner

The project I built in Baltimore covered a two-and-a-half year span. I probably went down there thirty times before anything was fabricated and worked on the site with sticks, strings, anything that established planes and distances for me. When they felt right in relation to existing elements, I measured them and they were drawn and engineered by others.

It is very seldom that I'm not involved in the fabrication and construction of these things. And I'm normally working with people who are much more skilled than the particular crafts involved. There are many people involved with me who are craftsmen and builders in their own right and who, on their own time, make very beautiful things that are the result of their own intentions. It's analogous to the theater or dance. If something works, it's because of the interaction of all of us.

Lois Tarlow, "Alternative Space: Richard Fleischner," interview, *Art New England* 4 (April 1983): 15.

Andy Goldsworthy

I have become aware of how nature is in a state of change, and that change is the key to understanding. I want my art to be sensitive and alert to changes in material, season and weather.

A rock is not independent of its surroundings. The way it sits tells how it came to be there. The energy and space around a rock is as important as the energy and space within. The weather; rain, sun, snow, hail, mist, calm, is that external space made visible. When I touch a rock, I am touching and working the space around it. In an effort to understand why that rock is there and where it is going I do not take it away from the area in which I found it.

Sometimes a work is at its best when most threatened by the weather. A balanced rock is given enormous tension and force by a wind that might cause its collapse. I have worked with colourful leaves, delicate grasses and feathers made extra vivid by a dark rain-laden sky that cast no shadow. Had it rained the work would have become mud-splattered and washed away.

I make one or two pieces of work each day I go out. From a month's work two or three pieces are successful. The "mistakes" are very important. Each new work is a result of knowledge accumulated through past work. A good work is the result of being in the right place at the right time with the right material.

Letter to the author, June 14, 1983.

Nancy Holt

My work also is about putting function back into art. I want to emphasize that I'm tired of the isolation of aesthetics. There has been a lot of aestheticizing going on, and it was very much part of the Conceptual Art movement—there were artists during the sixties who would go around and select things in the environment saying that they were works of art, or take photographs of them so that they could be transformed into art. So, there was a whole movement to aestheticise the environment.

Right along some of my work has had a functional aspect, like indicating sun cycles or astronomical alignments, and with the park I'm working on now in Washington, D.C. I have to think about people sitting down and having enough room for baby carriages and so on. So by doing that I'm making art more functional. Art needs to be a more necessary part of the world, of society.

From an interview with Nancy Holt in Micky Donnelly, *Circa* (Belfast) 11 (July–August 1983), p. 9.

Maya Lin

The worst thing in the world would have been indifference to my piece. The monument may lack an American flag, but you're surrounded by America, by the Washington Monument and the Lincoln Memorial. I don't design pure objects like those. I work with the landscape, and I hope that the object and the land are equal players.

The piece itself is apolitical in the sense that it doesn't comment directly on the war—only on the men that died. For some people—especially right-wing politicians—that's political enough. It's like the emperor's new clothes. What people see, or don't see is their own projection.

Classical Greek temples were never white. They were highly colored. At some point much later, someone decided that white signified classical architecture. Black for me is a lot more peaceful and gentle than white. White marble may be very beautiful, but you can't read anything on it. I wanted something that would be soft on the eyes, and turn into a mirror if you polished it. The point is to see yourself reflected in the names. Also the mirror image doubles and triples the space. I thought black was a beautiful color and appropriate for the design.

In a world of phallic memorials that rise upwards, the memorial certainly does have a female sensibility. I didn't set out to conquer the earth, or overpower it, the way Western man usually does. I don't think I've made a passive piece, but neither is it a memorial to the idea of war.

Elizabeth Hess, "A Tale of Two Memorials," p. 123.

David Nash

Earlier, I used woodmill wood, regular standard units; later, greenwood, fresh from the tree; now, the tree itself. The more I look at the tree, the more I see the tree: Its space and location, its volume and structure, its engineering and balance. More than that, I see the uniqueness of each single tree, and beyond that still I see it as a great emblem of life. A potent vibrant tower, a whirling prayer wheel of natural energy.

Fletched Over Ash, n.p., published on the occasion of Nash's exhibition at AIR Gallery, London, 1978.

James Pierce

I find that earthworking is an economical and relatively harmless means of satisfying desires for control, security and immortality while reliving the history of the race and discovering one's humanity in physical union with nature.

My work is always tempered by the "genius of the place," as Alexander Pope would say. I work with the landscape, not against it. This is not only true in a visual sense, but my medium is the landscape itself, its earth, rocks, and trees. I work in these materials because I feel their elemental power and because they cost nothing and are long lasting. I accept them as they are and do not alter their basic nature. The earthworks are literally alive with insects, birds and even an occasional mammal. These lifeforms add an everchanging variety of color, texture, and movement to an underlying simplicity of form. The discipline imposed by this essential simplicity is a constant spur to invention, as the original stimulus is sometimes surprisingly altered to satisfy requirements of support, slope, drainage, and exposure. In earthworking, unlike painting, not everything is possible. You know when to stop.

Letter to the author, November 8, 1976.

Robert Smithson

Across the country there are many mining areas, disused quarries and polluted lakes and rivers. One practical solution for the utilization of such devastated places would be land and water re-cycling in terms of "earth art." Recently, when I was in Holland, I worked in a sand quarry that was slated for redevelopment. The Dutch are especially aware of the physical landscape. A dialectic between land reclamation and mining usage must be established. The artist and the miner must become conscious of themselves as natural agents. In effect, this extends to all kinds of mining and building. When the miner or builder loses sight of what he is doing through the abstractions of technology he cannot practically cope with necessity. The world needs coal and highways, but we do not need the results of strip-mining or highway trusts. Economics, when abstracted from

135

the world, is blind to natural processes. Art can become a resource, that mediates between the ecologist and the industrialist. Ecology and industry are not one-way streets, rather they should be cross-roads. Art can help to provide the needed dialectic between them. A lesson can be learned from the Indian cliff dwellings and earthworks mounds. Here we see nature and necessity in consort.

"Untitled, 1971," in Nancy Holt, ed., *The Writings of Robert Smithson*, p. 220.

James Turrell

Roden Crater Project

You can note, when standing on an open plain, that the sky is not limitless and has a definable shape and a sense of enclosure, often referred to as celestial vaulting. Then, when lying down, you can note a difference in the sense of shape. Clearly, these limits are malleable. To work with the limits of the space of the sky and its sense of interior sizing, a hemispherically shaped, dished space, about 400 to 1000 feet above a plain, was sought. It was necessary that this space be on a plain so that some preliminary sense of celestial vaulting could be experienced. A crater-shaped space was desired so that it could be formed to effect changes in the perception of the size and shape of the sky. The

height above the plain was important, so that the slight quality of concave curvature to the earth experienced by pilots at low altitudes would increase the sense of celestial vaulting after you emerged from the crater space. A high-altitude site with infrequent cloud cover was also sought, so that the deeper blue of the sky could be utilized to support a close-in sense of celestial vaulting while in the bottom of the crater. Either a solitary cinder cone or a butte would satisfy these requirements.

All the Western states were flown, looking for possible sites. The search itself altered many ideas regarding the piece and also generated ideas for future works. Roden Crater, a volcano on the edge of the Painted Desert, was decided upon. The form of the volcano and its surroundings also changed my thinking about the piece. Obviously, this particular geological feature was selected not only because it met the requirements for the work, but also because the volcano itself is a powerful entity.

Rather than impose a plan upon the landscape, it was decided to work in phase with the surroundings. The site is a volcano, and will remain so. But it will be worked enough so that the desired experience will be heightened and ordered. This could also allow the piece to exist without beginning or end.

James Turrell: Light and Space, p. 42.

LOCATIONS OF SELECTED WORKS

Unless otherwise indicated, all works are accessible to the public.

Carl Andre. *Stone Field Sculpture*, 1977. Hartford Public Green, Main and Gold Streets, Hartford, Connecticut.

Herbert Bayer. *Earth Mound* and *Marble Garden*, 1955. Aspen Meadows, Aspen Institute for Humanistic Studies, Aspen, Colorado.
——. *Anderson Park*, 1973. Aspen Institute for Humanistic Studies, Aspen, Colorado.
——. *Mill Creek Canyon Earthworks*, 1982. Mill Creek Canyon Park, Titus and Canyon Streets, Kent, Washington.

William Bennett. *Jamesville Quarry Sculpture*, work in progress. Jamesville, New York. For additional information, contact the artist at Department of Fine Arts, University of Virginia, Charlottesville, Virginia 22903.

Walter De Maria. *Las Vegas Piece*, 1969. For information, contact Dia Art Foundation, 141 Wooster Street, #3A, New York, New York 10012.
——. *The Lightning Field*, 1971–77. To arrange a visit, write Dia Art Foundation, Box 207, Quemado, New Mexico 87829.

Stan Dolega. Reclamation project, 1981. One-half mile east of Hanna, Wyoming, off Wyoming Highway 30 (follow signs to the city dump).

Ian Hamilton Finlay. *Stonypath*, begun 1967. *Stonypath* is open by appointment between May and September. Write to Stonypath, Dunsyre, Lanarkshire, Scotland.
——. *Five Columns for the Kröller-Müller*, 1981. In the garden of the Rijksmuseum Kröller-Müller, Otterlo, the Netherlands.

Harvey Fite. *Opus 40*, 1939–76. For directions and a schedule of open days, write Friends of Opus 40, 7480 Fite Road, Saugerties, New York 12477.

Richard Fleischner. *Sod Maze*, 1974. On the grounds of Château-sur-Mer, Bellevue Avenue, Newport, Rhode Island.
——. *Chain Link Maze*, 1978. Stadium Drive, University of Massachusetts, Amherst.
——. *Cow Island Project*, 1978. Roger Williams Park, Ninth and Elmwood Avenue, Providence, Rhode Island.
——. *Baltimore Project*, 1980. Social Security Administration Center, 6401 Security Boulevard, Woodlawn, Maryland.

Michael Heizer. *Double Negative*, 1969–70. *Double Negative* is reached by driving north from Overton, Nevada, to the Overton airport. There, bear right onto a road which, after about two miles, climbs steeply up the western escarpment of the Mormon Mesa. Drive about three miles to nearly the other side of the mesa. Just before the road makes a 90-degree turn to the right and drops down the far side of the mesa, another road diagonals off to the left. Bear left on this road, which leads northeast slightly over a mile to *Double Negative*. There are other tracks which cross this last road, so this section of the trip can be confusing. *Double Negative* is in the third scallop of the escarpment north of where the road drops down the eastern edge of the mesa. See USGS map "Overton Quadrangle," 15-minute series.
——. *Complex One City*, 1972–76. For further information on this work, contact Xavier Fourcade, Inc., 36 East 75th Street, New York, New York 10021.
——. *Adjacent, Against, Upon*, 1976. Myrtle Edwards Park, Alaskan Way between West Bay and West Thomas, Seattle, Washington.
——. *This Equals That*, 1980. State Capitol Complex, Lansing, Michigan.
——. *Levitated Mass*, 1983. IBM Corporation, Madison Avenue at 56th Street, New York, New York.

Nancy Holt. *Sun Tunnels*, 1973–76. Lucin, Utah, the town nearest to *Sun Tunnels*, can be approached from the south by leaving Interstate 80 at Oasis, Nevada, and driving north on Route 30 through Montello. It can also be reached from the east by leaving Interstate 80N at Snowville, Utah, and heading west on Route 30 through Park Valley and Rosette. In either case, turn south off Route 30 about seventeen miles northeast of Montello (at "Grouse Creek Junction") onto a gravel road which leads four miles into Lucin. Continue south from Lucin two and one-half miles, then bear left, driving east. *Sun Tun-* nels should begin to be visible off to the right at this point. After two miles, bear right one-half mile to *Sun Tunnels*. See USGS maps "Lucin Quadrangle" and "Pigeon Mountain Quadrangle," 7.5-minute series.
——. *Rock Rings*, 1979. On the campus of Western Washington University, Bellingham, Washington.
——. *Star Crossed*, 1979–80. On the campus of Miami University, Oxford, Ohio.
——. *Annual Ring*, 1980–81. Federal Building, Saginaw, Michigan.
——. Rosslyn park project, work in progress. At the intersection of Fairfax and Fort Meyer drives, Rosslyn, Arlington, Virginia.

Robert Irwin. *Untitled (Filigreed Steel Line for Wellesley College)*, 1980. On the campus of Wellesley College, Wellesley, Massachusetts.
——. *Untitled*, 1980–81. Steel wall for East Portal Park, Carpenter Plaza, Dallas, Texas.

Joseph Kinnebrew. *Grand River Sculpture*, 1975. Bank of Grand River at 600 Front Street, N.W., Grand Rapids, Michigan.

Andrew Leicester. *Prospect V-III*, 1982. On the campus of Frostburg State College, Frostburg, Maryland. Write or call 301-689-4000 for open hours.

Maya Lin. *Vietnam Veterans Memorial*, 1982. Constitution Gardens, Constitution Avenue at 21st Street, N.W., Washington, D.C.

Robert Morris. *Observatory*, 1971; reconstructed 1977. *Observatory* is located along the road from Lelystad to Swifterbant, northeast of Amsterdam, the Netherlands. It is at the junction of Houtribweg and Swifteringweg about midway between the two towns. Maps and details on bus service from Amsterdam have been published in *Robert Morris's Observatory in Oostelijk Flevoland* by the Stedelijk Museum, Amsterdam, 1977.
——. *Grand Rapids Project*, 1973–74. Belknap Park, Coldbrook Road, Grand Rapids, Michigan.
——. Untitled reclamation project for King County, Washington, 1979. The site is ten miles south of Seattle and one-half mile east of Interstate 5 at the intersection of 40th Place South and South 216th Street. Exit I-5 at South

200th Street, turn east, follow Military Road to South 216th, and bear left.

Isamu Noguchi. *Marble Garden*, 1960–64. Beinecke Library, on the campus of Yale University, New Haven, Connecticut.

————. *Chase Manhattan Bank Plaza Garden*, 1961–64. Chase Manhattan Bank, 1 Chase Manhattan Plaza, New York, New York.

————. *Playscapes*, 1975. In Piedmont Park, Atlanta, Georgia.

————. *Landscape of Time*, 1975. Federal Building, 915 2nd Avenue, Seattle, Washington.

————. *Hart Plaza*, 1972–78. Jefferson and Auditorium Drive, Detroit, Michigan.

Beverly Pepper. *Amphisculpture*, 1974–77. On the grounds of the A T & T Corporation Headquarters, Routes 202/206 North, Bedminster, New Jersey.

James Pierce. *Pratt Farm*, begun 1970. For information on visiting Pierce's garden of history, write to the artist at the Department of Art, University of Kentucky, Lexington, Kentucky 40506.

Richard Serra. *Spin Out (For Robert Smithson)*, 1973. In the garden at the Rijksmuseum Kröller-Müller, Otterlo, the Netherlands.

————. *St. John's Rotary Arc*, 1980. In lower Manhattan at Hudson, Ericsson, Varick, and Laight Street.

Robert Smithson. *Spiral Jetty*, 1970. Spiral Jetty is reached by driving west from Brigham City, Utah, on Route 84. At Corrine, about five miles west of Brigham City, bear left onto Route 83. Continue for about eighteen miles to Lampo Junction, and bear left toward Promontory and the Golden Spike National Historic Site. Continue west on a dirt road down Promontory Hollow after passing the Golden Spike Historic Site. About six miles west of the historic site, as Promontory Hollow begins to open up onto Rozel Flat, the road will fork. Bear left about a mile and a half to another fork ("Pipeline Point"). Bear right, and drive across Rozel Flat toward the Great Salt Lake, which will begin to be visible in the distance between Promontory Mountains on the left and Rozel Hills on the right. The road will curve around the east side of the Rozel Hills and end at an abandoned oil drilling site marked by a straight jetty. *Spiral Jetty* is a mile up the shore to the right from there, and can be reached on foot or on a very rough road just up the hill from the drilling site. It is a total of about fifteen miles from the historic site to *Spiral Jetty*. See USGS map "Great Salt Lake City and Vicinity." As *Spiral Jetty* is often submerged, it is advisable to check with the Chamber of Commerce in Brigham City before going to the site to determine if the water is above the 1970 level.

Athena Tacha. *Streams*, 1976. On the banks of Plum Creek, Vine Street Park, Oberlin, Ohio.

James Turrell. *Roden Crater Project*, work in progress. For further information, contact the Skystone Foundation, Box 725, Flagstaff, Arizona 86002.

SELECTED BIBLIOGRAPHY

This is a concise rather than an exhaustive listing. Individual bibliographies for those artists discussed at length in the text follow the general one. Sources that discuss more than one artist are included in the general bibliography and are not repeated in the individual listings. The general bibliography includes books, exhibition catalogs, and periodicals. Special issues of periodicals that include more than one essay on the subject are listed under the title of the issue or the name of the special editor; individual essays within such issues are not also listed by author. The general bibliography also contains some pertinent monographic essays on artists discussed briefly or not at all in the text.

General

Alloway, Lawrence. "Site Inspection." Artforum 15 (October 1976): 49–55.

Anderson, Wayne. American Sculpture in Process: 1930–1970. Boston: New York Graphic Society, 1975.

Auping, Michael. Common Ground: Five Artists in the Florida Landscape, exhibition catalog. Sarasota: John and Mable Ringling Museum of Art, 1982. Includes Hamish Fulton, Helen and Newton Harrison, Michael Singer, and Alan Sonfist.

"Art Outdoors," special issue. Studio International 193 (March–April 1977): 82–130. Includes essays by Lucy R. Lippard, Nancy D. Rosen, and Andrew Causey.

Baker, Elizabeth. "Artworks on the Land." Art in America 64 (January–February 1976): 92–96.

Beardsley, John. Probing the Earth: Contemporary Land Projects, exhibition catalog. Washington, D.C.: Smithsonian Institution Press, 1977. Published for the Hirshhorn Museum and Sculpture Garden.

———. Art in Public Places: A Survey of Community-Sponsored Projects Supported by the National Endowment for the Arts. Washington, D.C.: Partners for Livable Places, 1981.

———. "Personal Sensibilities in Public Places." Artforum 19 (Summer 1981): 43–45.

Bongartz, Roy. "It's Called Earth Art — and Boulderdash." New York Times Magazine, February 1, 1970, pp. 16–17, 22–30.

Bourdon, David. "What on Earth!" Life 66 (April 25, 1969): 80–86. A report on Cornell's Earth Art exhibition.

Burnham, Jack. Great Western Salt Works. New York: George Braziller, 1974.

Castle, Ted. "Art in Its Place." Geo 4 (September 1982): 64–75, 112.

Celant, Germano. Arte Povera. New York: Praeger Publishers, 1969.

Clay, Grady. "Earthworks Move Upstage." Landscape Architecture 70 (January 1980): 55–57. Report on Seattle earthworks project.

"Discussions with Heizer, Oppenheim, Smithson." Avalanche, no. 1 (Fall 1970), pp. 48–71.

Earth Art, exhibition catalog. Ithaca: Andrew Dickson White Museum, Cornell University, 1970. Includes essays by William C. Lipke, Willoughby Sharp.

"Earth Movers." Time 92 (October 11, 1968): 84. Review of Dwan Gallery Earthworks exhibition.

Earthworks: Land Reclamation as Sculpture, exhibition catalog. Seattle: Seattle Art Museum, 1979. A project of the King County Arts Commission; essay by Robert Morris.

Foote, Nancy. "The Anti-Photographers." Artforum 15 (September 1976): 46–54.

———. "Monument-Sculpture-Earthwork." Artforum 18 (October 1979): 32–37. Report on the Seattle earthworks project.

Forgey, Ben. "Art Out of Nature Which Is About Nothing But Nature: Work of Michael Singer." Smithsonian 8 (January 1978): 62–64.

———. "You Can Range-Ride or Rope a Steer in This Work of Art." Smithsonian 14 (December 1983): 134–43. Report on Alan Wood's Ranch project.

Friedman, Bruce Jay. "Dirty Pictures." Esquire 75 (May 1971): 42, 112–17.

Gabriel, Bertram. "Works of Earth." Horizon 25 (January–February 1982): 42–48.

Glueck, Grace. "Art in Public Places Stirs Widening Debate." New York Times, May 23, 1982, section 2, pp. 1, 30.

———. "Serving the Environment." New York Times, June 27, 1982, section 2, pp. 25–26. Recent public environmental artworks.

Gottschalk, Earl C., Jr. "Earth-shaking News from the Art World: Sculpturing the Land." Wall Street Journal, September 10, 1976, pp. 1, 19.

"Helen and Newton Harrison," special section. Arts Magazine 52 (February 1978): 126–33. Essays by Kim Levin, Peter Selz, and Kristine Stiles.

Herrera, Hayden. "City Earthwork." Art in America 64 (September 1976): 100–101. Suzanne Harris's Locus Up One.

Hicky, Dave. "Earthscapes, Landworks and Oz." Art in America 59 (September–October 1971): 40–49.

Hobbs, Robert, ed. "Earthworks: Past and Present," special issue. Art Journal 42 (Fall 1982): 191–233. Includes nine essays.

Howett, Catherine. "New Directions in Environmental Art." Landscape Architecture 67 (January 1977): 38–46.

Johnson, Ellen H. "Nature as Source in Athena Tacha's Art." Artforum 19 (January 1981): 58–62.

Junker, Howard. "The New Sculpture: Getting Down to the Nitty Gritty." Saturday Evening Post 241 (November 2, 1968): 42–47.

Kardon, Janet. "Janet Kardon Interviews Some Modern Maze-Makers." Art International 20 (April–May 1976): 64–68.

Kepes, Gyorgy, ed. Arts of the Environment. New York: George Braziller, 1972.

Kern, Hermann. "Labyrinths: Tradition and Contemporary Works." Artforum 19 (May 1981): 60–68.

Kingsley, April. "Six Women at Work in the Landscape." Arts Magazine 52 (April 1978): 108–12.

Krauss, Rosalind. Passages in Modern Sculpture. London: Thames and Hudson; New York: Viking, 1977.

———. "Sculpture in the Expanded Field." October, no. 8 (Spring 1979), pp. 31–44.

"Landscape Sculpture: The New Leap," special issue. Landscape Architecture 61 (July 1971): 296–343. Includes editorial by Grady Clay, essays by Richard Koshalek, James Wines.

Larson, Kay. "New Landscapes in Art." New York Times Magazine, May 13, 1979, pp. 20–23, 28–38.

———. "The Expulsion from the Garden: Environmental Sculpture at the Winter Olympics." Artforum 18 (April 1980): 36–45.

Leider, Philip. "How I Spent My Summer Vacation, or, Art and Politics in Nevada, Berkeley, San Francisco and Utah." Artforum 9 (September 1970): 40–49.

Linker, Kate. "George Trakas and the Syntax of Space." *Arts Magazine* 50 (January 1976): 92–94.

———. "Public Sculpture: The Pursuit of the Pleasurable and Profitable Paradise." *Artforum* 19 (March 1981): 64–73. "Public Sculpture II: Provisions for the Paradise." *Artforum* 19 (Summer 1981): 37–42.

Lippard, Lucy R. "Complexes: Architectural Sculpture in Nature." *Art in America* 67 (January–February 1979): 86–97.

———. "Gardens: Some Metaphors for a Public Art." *Art in America* 69 (November 1981): 136–50.

———. *Overlay: Contemporary Art and the Art of Prehistory*. New York: Pantheon Books, 1983.

Masheck, Joseph. "The Panama Canal and Some Other Works of Work." *Artforum* 9 (May 1971): 38–42.

McFadden, Sarah. "Report from Lake Placid. The Big Secret: Art at the Olympics." *Art in America* 68 (April 1980): 53–63.

Müller, Gregoire. *The New Avant-Garde: Issues for the Art of the Seventies*. New York: Praeger Publishers, 1972. Photographs by Gianfranco Gorgoni.

Noah, Barbara. "Cost-Effective Earth Art." *Art in America* 68 (January 1980): 12–15. Report on the Seattle earthworks project.

Onorato, Ronald J. "The Modern Maze." *Art International* 20 (April–May 1976): 21–25.

Pepper, Beverly, with Butterfield, Jan. "Beverly Pepper: A Space Has Many Aspects." *Arts Magazine* 50 (September 1975): 91–94. Interview.

Reuterswärd, Patrik. "The Quarries of William Bennett." *Konsthistorisk tidskrift* 51 (Stockholm, 1982): 143–46.

"Richard Serra," special section. *Arts Magazine* 55 (November 1980): 118–33. Includes interview with Douglas Crimp, essay by Donald Kuspit, journal by Robert Pincus-Witten.

Rosenberg, Harold. *The De-definition of Art: Action Art to Pop to Earthworks*. New York: Horizon Press, 1972.

———. *Art on the Edge: Creators and Situations*. New York: Macmillan Publishing, 1975.

Sheffield, Margaret. "Natural Structures: Michael Singer's Sculpture and Drawings." *Artforum* 17 (February 1979): 48–51.

Tacha, Athena. "Rhythm as Form." *Landscape Architecture* 68 (May 1978): 196–205.

Tillim, Sidney. "Earthworks and the New Picturesque." *Artforum* 7 (December 1968): 42–45.

Tomkins, Calvin. *The Scene: Reports on Post-Modern Art*. New York: Viking Press, 1976.

———. "The Art World: Like Water in a Glass." *New Yorker* 59 (March 21, 1983): 92–97. Report on recent public environmental artworks.

Tousley, Nancy. "Natural Hierarchy of Ma-

terials: An Interview with George Trakas." *Artscanada* 36 (August–September 1979): 24–26.

Urban Encounters: Art, Architecture, Audience, exhibition catalog. Philadelphia: Institute of Contemporary Art, University of Pennsylvania, 1980. Essays by Janet Kardon, Lawrence Alloway, Ian L. McHarg, and Nancy Foote.

Wortz, Melinda. "Surrendering to Presence: Robert Irwin's Esthetic Integration." *Artforum* 20 (November 1981): 63–65.

Herbert Bayer

Bayer, Herbert. *Herbert Bayer: Painter, Designer, Architect*. New York: Reinhold Publishing, 1967.

Herbert Bayer: A Total Concept, exhibition catalog. Denver: Denver Art Museum, 1973.

Herbert Bayer: From Type to Landscape. Designs, Projects and Proposals, 1923–73, exhibition catalog. Hanover: Dartmouth College Museum and Galleries, 1977. Text by Jan van der Marck.

Constantin Brancusi

Brezianu, Barbu. *Brancusi in Romania*. Bucharest: Editura Academiei Republicii Socialiste Romania, 1976.

Geist, Sidney. *Brancusi: A Study of the Sculpture*. New York: Grossman, 1968.

———. *Brancusi: The Kiss*. New York: Harper and Row, 1978.

Jianou, Ionel, and Noica, Constantin. *Introduction à la sculpture de Brancusi*. Paris: Arted, 1976. Chapter 5: "L'Ensemble monumental de Targu-Jiu," pp. 53–71.

Miller, Sanda. "Brancusi's 'Column of the Infinite.'" *Burlington Magazine* 122 (July 1980): 470–80.

Noguchi, Isamu. "Noguchi on Brancusi." *Craft Horizons* 36 (August 1976): 26–29.

Tucker, William. "Brancusi at Tirgu-Jiu." *Studio International* 184 (October 1972): 117–21.

———. *Early Modern Sculpture*. New York: Oxford University Press, 1974. Chapter 7: "Brancusi at Tirgu Jiu," pp. 129–43.

Christo

Bourdon, David. *Christo*. New York: Harry N. Abrams (1972).

Christo: Valley Curtain. New York: Harry N. Abrams (1973). Photographs by Harry Shunk.

Christo's Running Fence. New York: Harry N. Abrams (1978). Photographs by Gianfranco Gorgoni, preface by Calvin Tomkins, captions by David Bourdon.

Fineberg, Jonathan. "Theater of the Real: Thoughts on Christo." *Art in America* 67 (December 1979): 92–99.

Frankenstein, Alfred. "Christo's 'Fence,' Beauty or Betrayal?" *Art in America* 64 (November–December 1976): 58–61.

Ratcliff, Carter. "Unwrapping Christo." *Saturday Review* 7 (December 1980): 18–22.

Spies, Werner, and Volz, Wolfgang, photo-

graphs. *The Running Fence Project: Christo*. New York: Harry N. Abrams, 1977.

Tomkins, Calvin. "Onward and Upward with the Arts: Running Fence." *New Yorker* 53 (March 28, 1977): 43–46.

Walter De Maria

Adrian, Dennis. "Walter De Maria: Word and Thing." *Artforum* 5 (January 1967): 28–29.

Beardsley, John. "Art and Authoritarianism: Walter De Maria's Lightning Field." *October*, no. 16 (Spring 1981), pp. 35–38.

Bourdon, David. "Walter De Maria: The Singular Experience." *Art International* 12 (December 20, 1968): 39–43, 72.

De Maria, Walter. "The Lightning Field." *Artforum* 18 (April 1980): 51–59.

"High Priest of Danger." *Time* 93 (May 2, 1969): 54.

Leder, Dennis. "Walter De Maria: Mounds, Mines, Markers." *America* 142 (March 15, 1980): 219–20.

Wortz, Melinda. "Walter De Maria's 'Lightning Field.'" *Arts Magazine* 54 (May 1980): 170–73.

Ian Hamilton Finlay

Bann, Stephen. "A Description of Stonypath." *Journal of Garden History* 1 (April–June 1981): 113–44.

Brown, David. "Stonypath: An Inland Garden." *Studio International* 193 (January–February 1977): 34–37.

McIntosh, Christopher. "A Garden of Many Dimensions: Stonypath, Lanarks." *Country Life* 162 (October 6, 1977): 928–30.

Nature Over Again After Poussin: Some Discovered Landscapes, exhibition catalog. Glasgow: Collins Exhibition Hall, University of Strathclyde, 1980. Essay by Stephen Bann; "Unconnected Sentences on Gardening" by Ian Hamilton Finlay.

Selected Ponds. Reno: West Coast Poetry Review, 1975. Photographs of Stonypath by Dave Paterson, essays by Stephen Bann and Bernard Lassus.

Harvey Fite

Brandau, Robert, and Ward, Eleanor. "Stone Upon Stone: The Craft of Dry Stone Masonry." *Historic Preservation* 27 (April–June 1975): 26–29.

Kent, Norman. "A Sculptor's Quarry." *American Artist* 22 (January 1958): 25–31.

McFadden, Sarah. "Going Places, Part II: The Outside Story. Opus 40." *Art in America* 68 (Summer 1980): 52–54.

"Opus 40: Mysticism in Stone." *House and Garden Building Guide* (Fall–Winter 1976–77), pp. 110–11.

"The Quarrymaster of Saugerties." *Artnews* 76 (October 1977): 23–24, 26.

"Sculptor Nearing an End to a Massive 40-Year Task at an Abandoned Quarry." *New York Times*, August 3, 1968, p. 27.

Richard Fleischner

Davies, Hugh. "Richard Fleischner's Sculpture of the Past Decade." *Arts Magazine* 51 (April 1977): 118–23.

———, and Jordy, William H., preface. *Richard Fleischner*, exhibition catalog. Amherst: University Gallery, University of Massachusetts, 1977.

Onorato, Ronald J. "Reviews: Richard Fleischner." *Artforum* 16 (November 1977): 70–71. Cow Island project.

———. "Richard Fleischner's Baltimore Project." *Arts Magazine* 56 (October 1981): 64–67.

Hamish Fulton

Auping, Michael. "Hamish Fulton: Moral Landscapes." *Art in America* 71 (February 1983): 87–93.

"Hamish Fulton." In *Landscape: Theory*. New York: Lustrum Press, 1980, pp. 77–93. Includes the text of an interview with Peter Turner.

Michael Heizer

Davis, Douglas. "The Earth Mover." *Newsweek* 84 (November 18, 1974): 113.

Gruen, John. "Michael Heizer: You Might Say I'm in the Construction Business." *Artnews* 79 (December 1977): 96–99.

Heizer, Michael. "The Art of Michael Heizer." *Artforum* 8 (December 1969): 32–39.

Michael Heizer, exhibition catalog. Essen: Museum Folkwang; Otterlo: Rijksmuseum Kröller-Müller, 1979.

Michael Heizer/Actual Size, exhibition catalog. Detroit: Detroit Institute of Arts, 1971.

Waldman, Diane. "Holes without History." *Artnews* 70 (May 1971): 44–48, 66–68.

Yau, John. "Sculpture as Archaeology." *Vogue* 171 (August 1981): 290–93, 347.

Nancy Holt

Castle, Ted. "Nancy Holt: Siteseer." *Art in America* 70 (March 1982): 84–91.

Forgey, Benjamin. "A Park Grows in Rosslyn." *Washington Post*, September 17, 1983, pp. C1, C2.

Holt, Nancy. "Sun Tunnels." *Artforum* 15 (April 1977): 32–37.

———. "Stone Enclosure: Rock Rings." *Arts Magazine* 53 (June 1979): 152–55.

Rosenberg, Avis Lang, and Keziere, Robert. "Stone Enclosure: Rock Rings." *Vanguard* 8 (February 1979): 22–27.

Maya Lin

Forgey, Benjamin. "Model of Simplicity." *Washington Post*, November 14, 1981, pp. C1, 4.

———. "A Solution with Pride, Harmony and Vision." *Washington Post*, February 9, 1983, pp. F1, 4.

Hess, Elizabeth. "A Tale of Two Memorials." *Art in America* 71 (April 1983): 120–27.

McCombs, Phil. "The Memorial's Moment of Truce." *Washington Post*, February 9, 1983, pp. F1, 6.

Sorkin, Michael. "What Happens When a Woman Designs a War Monument?" *Vogue* 173 (May 1983): 120, 122.

Richard Long

Compton, Michael. *Some Notes on the Work of Richard Long*. London: British Council, 1976. Published on the occasion of Long's exhibition at the Thirty-seventh Venice Biennale.

Field, Simon. "Touching the Earth: Simon Field Examines the Work of Richard Long." *Art and Artists* 8 (April 1973): 14–19.

Foote, Nancy. "Long Walks." *Artforum* 18 (Summer 1980): 42–47.

Fuchs, R. H. "Memories of Passing: A Note on Richard Long." *Studio International* 187 (April 1974): 172–73.

"Nineteen Stills from the Work of Richard Long." *Studio International* 179 (March 1970): 106–11.

Robert Morris

Grand Rapids Project: Robert Morris. Grand Rapids: Grand Rapids Art Museum, 1975.

Morris, Robert. "Aligned with Nazca." *Artforum* 14 (October 1975): 26–39.

———. "The Present Tense of Space." *Art in America* 66 (January–February 1978): 70–81.

———. "Notes on Art as/and Land Reclamation." *October*, no. 12 (Spring 1980), pp. 87–102.

Robert Morris's Observatory in Oostelijk Flevoland. Amsterdam: Stedelijk Museum, 1977.

Robert Morris/Projects, exhibition catalog. Philadelphia: Institute of Contemporary Art, University of Pennsylvania, 1974.

Robert Morris: Selected Works, 1970–1981, exhibition catalog. Houston: Contemporary Arts Museum, 1981.

David Nash

Adams, Hugh. "The Woodman." *Art and Artists* 13 (April 1979): 44–47.

Hughes, Robert. "From Sticks to Cenotaphs." *Time* 115 (February 11, 1980): 65.

McPherson, Alan. "Interview with David Nash." *Artscribe*, no. 12 (June 1978), pp. 30–34.

Sixty Seasons: David Nash, exhibition catalog. Glasgow: Third Eye Centre, 1983. Essay by Hugh Adams.

Waldman, Diane. *British Art Now: An American Perspective*, exhibition catalog, pp. 80–99. New York: Solomon R. Guggenheim Museum, 1980.

Wood Quarry: David Nash, Otterlo 1982, exhibition catalog. Otterlo: Rijksmuseum Kröller-Müller, 1982.

Isamu Noguchi

Friedman, Martin. *Noguchi's Imaginary Landscapes*, exhibition catalog. Minneapolis: Walker Art Center, 1978. Environmental and stage designs.

Grove, Nancy, and Botnick, Diane. *The Sculpture of Isamu Noguchi, 1924–79*. New York: Garland Publishing, 1980. Catalog raisonné.

Hunter, Sam. *Isamu Noguchi*. New York: Abbeville Press, 1978.

Noguchi, Isamu, and Fuller, R. Buckminster, foreword. *A Sculptor's World*. New York: Harper and Row, 1968. Autobiography.

———, and Armstrong, Thomas, foreword. *Isamu Noguchi: The Sculpture of Spaces*, exhibition catalog. New York: Whitney Museum of American Art, 1980. Environmental projects and theater sets.

James Pierce

Beardsley, John. "James Pierce and the Picturesque Landscape." *Art International* 23 (November–December 1979): 6–15.

Pierce, James. "The Pratt Farm Turf Maze." *Art International* 20 (April–May 1976): 25–27.

———. *Pratt Farm: Garden of History*, exhibition catalog. Macon, Ga.: Mercer University, 1976.

Charles Ross

Ross, Charles. "Sunlight Convergence/Solar Burn." *Arts Magazine* 47 (December 1972–January 1973): 48–50.

———. *Sunlight Convergence/Solar Burn: The Equinoctial Year, September 23, 1971–September 22, 1972*. Salt Lake City: University of Utah Press and Art Department, 1976.

The Substance of Light: Sunlight Dispersion, The Solar Burns, Point Source/Star Space. Selected Works of Charles Ross, exhibition catalog. La Jolla: La Jolla Museum of Contemporary Art, 1976.

Charles Simonds

Abadie, Daniel. *Charles Simonds* (Art/Cahier 2). Paris: SMI, 1975.

Beardsley, John. "Charles Simonds: Extending the Metaphor." *Art International* 22 (February 1979): 14–19, 34.

Castle, Ted. "Charles Simonds: The New Adam." *Art in America* 71 (February 1983): 94–103.

Linker, Kate. "Charles Simonds' Emblematic Architecture." *Artforum* 17 (March 1979): 32–37.

Lippard, Lucy, and Simonds, Charles. "Microcosm to Macrocosm/Fantasy World to Real World." *Artforum* 12 (February 1974): 36–39. Interview.

Molderings, Herbert. *Schwebende Städte und andere Architekturen* (Floating Cities and Other Architectures), exhibition catalog. Münster: Westfälischer Kunstverein, 1978.

Neff, John H. *Charles Simonds*, exhibition catalog. Chicago: Museum of Contemporary Art, 1981. Includes essays by Daniel Abadie and John Beardsley and "Three Peoples" by the artist.

Patton, Phil. "Charles Simonds' Lost Worlds." *Artnews* 82 (February 1983): 84–90.

Robert Smithson

Alloway, Lawrence. "Robert Smithson's Development." *Artforum* 11 (November 1972): 52–61.

Bear, Liza, and Holt, Nancy. "Robert Smithson's Amarillo Ramp." *Avalanche*, no. 8 (Summer–Fall 1973), pp. 16–21.

Hobbs, Robert. *Robert Smithson: Sculpture*. Ithaca: Cornell University Press, 1981. Includes essays by Lawrence Alloway, John Coplans, and Lucy R. Lippard.

Holt, Nancy, ed. *The Writings of Robert Smithson*. New York: New York University Press, 1979. Anthology of the artist's writings, published and unpublished.

Robert Smithson: Drawings, exhibition catalog. New York: New York Cultural Center, 1974. Essays by Susan Ginsburg and Joseph Masheck.

"Robert Smithson," special issue. *Arts Magazine* 52 (May 1978): 96–144. Includes fifteen essays on or tributes to Smithson.

"Robert Smithson's Spiral Jetty," special section. *Arts Magazine* 56 (October 1981): 68–88. Includes essays by Elizabeth C. Childs and Donald B. Kuspit.

James Turrell

Hughes, Robert. "Poetry Out of Emptiness." *Time* 117 (January 5, 1981): 81.

James Turrell: Light and Space, exhibition catalog. New York: Whitney Museum of American Art, 1980. Introduction by Melinda Wortz.

Larson, Kay. "Dividing the Light from the Darkness." *Artforum* 19 (January 1981): 30–33.

Light Projections and Light Spaces, exhibition catalog. Amsterdam: Stedelijk Museum, 1976.

Marmer, Nancy. "James Turrell: The Art of Deception." *Art in America* 69 (May 1981): 90–99.

Tomkins, Calvin. "The Talk of the Town: Light." *New Yorker* 56 (December 15, 1980): 29–31.

INDEX

Photography Credits

All photographic material was obtained directly from the collection or photographer indicated in the caption, except for the following (numbers refer to plates): Charles Adler, courtesy Seattle Art in Public Places Program: 109; Alinari/Art Resource, New York: 76; Paul Berizzi, courtesy New York City Department of Parks and Recreation: 7; Joel Breger: 106, 117, 118; Courtesy British Tourist Authority: 1, 61; Courtesy Bronx Historical Society: 4; Nancy Calderwood: 30; Courtesy Leo Castelli Gallery, New York: 20–22, 107; Colleen Chartier, Seattle: 89; John Cliett: cover, 59, 60; Courtesy Dallas Museum of Fine Arts: 99; Bevin Davies, courtesy Sperone Westwater Fischer, New York: 37; Courtesy Dia Art Foundation, New York (copyright 1969, Walter De Maria): 13; Harvey Dwight: 71; Courtesy Xavier Fourcade, New York: 9; Herbert George, New York: 78–80; Gianfranco Gorgoni/Contact Press Images, New York (copyright 1983): 8, 10, 11, 15–19; Andrew Griffiths: 75; John Hoge and Nancy Leahy: 90–93; Ellen H. Johnson: 111; Robert Keziere: frontispiece, 125–28; Balthazar Korab, Troy, Mich.: 100–102, 108; Martin Lowenfish, courtesy American Museum of Natural History, New York: 12; Wyatt McSpadden, courtesy Ant Farm: 24; Dolores Neuman, Washington, D.C.: 129–32; Dave Paterson: 70, 72–74, 77; Pebble Beach Company: 5, 6; Margaret Robinette, Public Art Trust, Dallas: 105; Courtesy Sperone Westwater Fischer, New York: 34–36; Copyright James Turrell: 32; Wolfgang Volz (copyright Christo/Running Fence Corporation): 25, 26, 123, 124; Gene D. Wiggins: 23; Dick Wiser: 31.